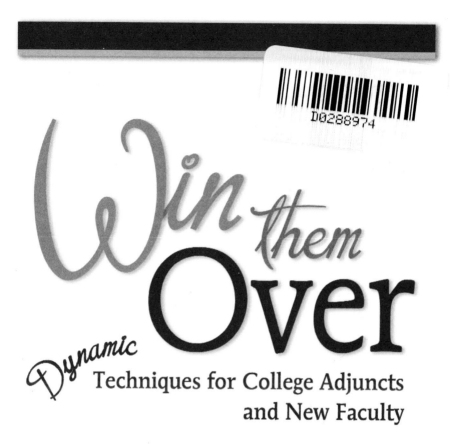

D0288974

# Win them Over

## Dynamic Techniques for College Adjuncts and New Faculty

### PATRICIA LINEHAN. Ph.D.

Atwood Publishing / Madison, WI

Win Them Over:
Dynamic Techniques for College Adjuncts and New Faculty
by Patricia Linehan, Ph.D

Copyright © 2007, Atwood Publishing
P.O. Box 3185
Madison, WI 53704

Cover and text illustrations by Karin Wrzesinski
Cover and text design © TLC Graphics, *www.TLCGraphics.com*

Library of Congress Cataloging-in-Publication Data

Linehan, Patricia, 1950-
  Win them over : dynamic techniques for college adjuncts and new
faculty / Patricia Linehan.
       p. cm.
  Includes bibliographical references.
  ISBN-13: 978-1-891859-67-0 (pbk.)
  1. College teachers—In-service training. 2. College teaching. I. Title.

  LB1738.L56 2006
  378.1'25--dc22
                                    2006025955

*Dedicated to my husband, Terry Clodfelter, Lt. Col. USAFRR,*
*who is a stellar college teacher and partner.*
*Thank you for helping with so many ideas and all your support.*

# Table of Contents

Why You Should Read This Book .............................. ix

Welcome to the World of Teaching...
and Hurry Up, Your Class Is About to Start! ..................... 1

Reality Check for Adjunct Instructors ......................... 3

Reality Check for New Full-time Instructors ..................... 5

Getting Ready to Teach ...................................... 7
   Questions You Need to Ask ...................................... 7
   Checklist: Getting Ready ......................................... 9

Course Design ............................................ 11
   Goals and Objectives First ....................................... 11
   Objectives and Bloom's Taxonomy ............................... 14
   Projects and Assignments and Bloom's Taxonomy ................... 17
   Textbooks and Ancillary Materials ............................... 17
   Pacing and Variety ............................................ 20
   Checklist: Course Design ...................................... 22

Course Management ...................................... 23
   Syllabus ..................................................... 23
   Schedule Table ............................................... 27
   Student Contact/Contract Sheet ................................. 29
   Organization: Class-in-a-Box .................................... 31
   No Surprises = Satisfaction .................................... 32
   Checklist: Course Management .................................. 33

**Grading Issues** ............................................. 35
  Scales ................................................... 35
  Privacy .................................................. 35
  Fairness in Grading ...................................... 36
  Grade Inflation .......................................... 37
  How Do You Grade Participation ........................... 38
  Checklist: Grading Issues ................................ 39

**Assessment** ............................................... 40
  Major Issues and Definitions ............................. 40
  Direct Measures of Student Learning ...................... 43
  Grading Rubrics: Formative and Summative Tools ........... 52
  Indirect Measures of Student Learning .................... 63
  Summative Indirect Measures .............................. 65
  Checklist: Assessment .................................... 69

**Motivating Students** ...................................... 70
  Expectancy–Value Theory .................................. 71
  Conceptions of Ability Theory ............................ 72
  Questions to Ask Yourself ................................ 73
  Incentives, Rewards, and a Little Punishment ............. 78
  Effective Teachers ....................................... 81

**Classroom Dynamics** ....................................... 82
  Getting Things Right at the Start ........................ 82
  "Troublemakers" and Troubled Students .................... 84
  Methods for Eliciting Questions .......................... 86
  Formats for Interaction .................................. 87
  Checklist: Motivation and Classroom Dynamics ............. 90

**Active Teaching and Learning** ............................. 92
  Helping Students Learn to Learn .......................... 92
  Memorizing ............................................... 94
  Mind Mapping ............................................. 95
  Teaching Critical Thinking Skills ........................ 96
  Dynamic Direct Instruction (Horror! A Lecture!) .......... 97
  Active Learning: The Philosophy and the Drawbacks ........ 100
  Grounding Principles ..................................... 102
  The Value of Images, Stories, and Fun .................... 103
  Critical Aspects of Good Active Learning Activities ...... 105
  Active Learning Technique One—Lecture Interrupting ....... 105

Active Learning Technique Two—Build It ........................ 106
Active Learning Technique Three—
    What Do You Think, Dr. Dewey? ........................... 108
Active Learning Technique Four—
    What Do You Think, Noted Panelists? ....................... 109
Active Learning Technique Five—Nominal Group ................ 110
Active Learning Technique Six—"Apply-Sheets" and Scenarios ........ 111
Active Learning Technique Seven—Multipurpose Activities .......... 113
Active Learning Technique Eight—Jigsaw Method ................ 114
Checklist: Active Teaching and Learning Techniques .............. 116

**Communication and Final Tips** .............................. **118**

**Final Words** ............................................. **121**

**Good Resources for Instructors** ............................. **122**

**About the Author** ........................................ **124**

# Why You Should Read This Book

First, because you want to be the best.

Second, because students want and deserve the best. Academic program reviews frequently measure quality of teaching by the number of terminal degrees held by faculty, but students measure quality of teaching quite differently. They *assume* that their instructor knows the subject; after all, they're paying to be taught by experts. They want *more than the degree;* they want invigorating, dynamic instruction that interests them and keeps them stretching, stimulated, updated, and very far from bored.

OK. Those are two good reasons to read this book. But maybe you want a practical reason.

You can't get more practical than this reason: *jobs*. Administrators know that quality of teaching influences retention. Great student evaluations can help you get more jobs (if you are an adjunct) or achieve tenure (if you are a new college instructor).

But good evaluations are not enough. All instructors in postsecondary institutions are expected to know about active learning techniques and alternative means of assessment. In other words, lectures and tests are no longer the way to go. Why not? Because we know that active techniques and frequent and varied means of assessment are critical in reaching all students, whatever their abilities and preparation and learning styles. That's why I emphasize them in this book.

The push for assessment and active learning is coming, not just from administrators, but also from accrediting agencies because of federal requirements that require them to include outcomes assessment in their standards. As a result, institutions must specify their educational goals and determine whether they are achieving those goals. The agencies are holding colleges accountable for the outcomes students get for their money.

When you are conversant in active learning techniques and alternative means of assessment, you are ahead of other instructors vying for positions you want. I've sat on lots of search committees and, believe me, we are easily impressed when candidates can both "talk" assessment and active learning and "walk" them too.

Few graduate degrees specifically teach you how to be a good instructor. But you can learn. Just keep reading!

### An Important Note

*Why doesn't this book have a lot of in-text citations and references within the manuscript?*

Because it isn't a research report on college teaching. It's a practical application of that research. (The research references on which this book is based are at the end.)

The goal here is simply to help you be a better teacher, immediately.

# Welcome to the World of Teaching...

### and Hurry Up, Your Class Is About to Start!

Whether you are an adjunct or a full-time new college instructor, welcome!

If you've had two or three months to prepare your classes, bravo! But chances are pretty good that you've had far less preparation time. New tenure-track hires are frequently too busy finishing their dissertations, hunting for a place to live, and moving to prepare classes in advance. Adjuncts are frequently notified late, so they have minimal time to prepare.

For my first adjunct position at a Big Ten research institution, I had only 12 days to prepare. I had never taught before. Any help I was expecting didn't materialize. My office was my car. I knew no one. I didn't have a clue what questions to ask. I was on my own with a textbook, an exceedingly sketchy sample syllabus, and memories of instructors I'd loved or hated.

The first day of class, my hands shook. I wanted to do a fabulous job, but I'm sure I was only average at best. I had the right degree and the right desire, but very few tools beyond the lecture and the test. That was a pretty standard toolkit 20 years ago, but now, as I mentioned earlier, lectures and tests are not enough.

After almost two decades in higher education as a teacher and administrator, I now know a lot more about teaching, assessment, and organization. I also know that quality teaching impacts how students think and feel about their college, which is a particular concern for administrators with retention figures in mind. Advertisements and search committees now emphasize knowledge of active learning and assessment.

But teaching was probably not the focus of your graduate degree. And a Master's or a Ph.D. is no guarantee that a person can teach—we've all suffered through brilliant Ph.D.s who simply couldn't explain their way out of a paper bag!

Our students are fairly demanding consumers. They do not appreciate straight lectures day after day, interrupted only by a midterm and a final. They expect learning environments to be crafted so all students have the opportunity to be engaged. Like it or not, that's the reality.

The other reality is this: In most fields there is a stack of applicants for each position. You must stand out to get your foot in the door—and once it is wedged in there, you have to be a good teacher to go to the next level. Luckily, teaching is both an art and a skill. The skill can be learned.

The little book in your hands is based on two things: long experience and educational psychology research. It is a book that truly would have helped me be a better instructor immediately, the first day on the job. I have written it to help new and adjunct instructors become absolutely stellar teachers, so their classes fill with students clamoring for their sections. Students want a dynamic, knowledgeable, intriguing instructor with a talent for inspiring her or his students. I want to help *you* be that instructor.

Teaching is the best job in the world! Enjoy and thrive!

— *Patricia L. Linehan*

# Reality Check for Adjunct Instructors

Personal contacts and relationships help you get first jobs. It's competitive out there. Market yourself. It's like fishing: you have to decide if you want to dangle one worm in the water or cast a big net. If adjunct teaching is a hobby, cast a worm. If you are doing this in order to pay rent and you want a full-time position, build multiple webs of relationships. That means:

- Don't *just* answer ads. Send resumes to *all* schools within commuting distance. Include great cover letters.

- Do follow-up phone calls asking to meet and talk with the VP, dean, or chair—whoever hires. (Your face and smile will come to mind for a last-minute "crisis hire.")

- After meeting, follow up with a thank-you note. Don't give up.

- Don't be a snob about where you'll teach. All teaching experience is helpful. The more types of colleges you teach at, the more you can honestly say you have experience with diverse groups.

- Seek out local instructors and administrators at conferences and chat. Establish relationships.

- Find out the hiring schedule for each school. Then, call before decisions are made.

- Let the hiring VP, dean, or chair know you are available on short notice, for "crisis hires." Remind them!

- Keep your contact information—e-mail address and phone number—updated so they can reach you.

- Answer calls immediately! For a last-minute hire, they are probably notifying three candidates. First come, first hired.

- When you send out a resume and cover letter, make sure they are flawless. I cannot tell you how many times I have been on search committees where poor proofreading sent an otherwise solid vita into the "look at last" pile. Right or wrong, that's reality.

- Personal contact also helps keep more adjunct classes coming your way. Keep in contact with your hiring authority. Don't be a pest, but be visible. If she or he invites you to a meeting or an in-service (professional development activities), go—and be sure to say hi! Many adjuncts are invited to in-services but few arrive. Be the exception.

- Personal contact helps you get a permanent job. Is there an all-faculty potluck on a night you'd rather stay home? Go! Who will be on the search committee if a position opens where you're an adjunct? Why, the faculty you've been chatting with in the copy room. The ability to demonstrate collegiality is an important factor in most hires.

- Students talk—about you and your teaching. Yes, they do—and you want it to be positive. I'm not talking about being "easy" so everyone likes you; that gets around negatively. I'm talking about being *good*. *So good, in fact, they tell everyone.*

# Reality Check for New Full-Time Instructors

You've landed the job—but there's no guarantee of tenure and job security. If you didn't ask during the hiring process, ask now about how tenure works at your college. Look at open tenure records and see what concerns the committees had, what questions the members asked, what the records of publishing, service, and teaching were like for those who succeeded and those who failed.

Use your time wisely to start building your tenure case now.

Choose only one or two committees, not 10, to serve on. You'll be too busy crafting your teaching and/or doing research and attempting to publish your research to do much service. If you can, choose the short, sweet service/committee assignments that give you a vita line but don't take three hours a week for the next 36 months. Keep good records of everything you do, including that sermon at your church and that freebie strategic planning facilitation for the YWCA.

Plan ahead. You already know from your dissertation process that institutional review boards sometimes work slowly, that research doesn't always go as planned, and that getting published in a reasonable and timely manner is next to impossible. You may be very tired from the dissertation process, but if the tenure expectations at your new college or university include research, you can't really take much of a break.

Use your dissertation to full advantage. Many tired graduates shelve their dissertation, knowing it wasn't the best work they can do; after all, it was a learning process. But this is a mistake. Use that dissertation to generate at least one article, hopefully several, and submit to smaller, less competitive journals.

Personal contacts and relationships help you keep jobs. It's competitive out there ... even after you get the job. Colleagues who genuinely like you and get to know you will recommend you for plum committees and are more likely to support you in general—during budget processes, for tenure, etc. You can't sit in your office and never talk with your colleagues and then expect them to actually care whether you get to stay or not ... no matter how wonderful your research. It's way too easy to get rid of an untenured colleague who's not collegial.

Avoid the petty political back-biting and conflicts that sometimes plague academia. Unfortunately, too many graduate students get a strong dose of this as a "hidden curriculum" during their Ph.D. work and fall right into the fray when they are hired. Please, try to rise above the forest of egos if you find yourself surrounded by them. Besides, at the beginning you don't know who has built alliances with whom, who used to date whom, etc. These are troubled waters and it's easy to drown. Stay maturely and safely on the sidelines.

Become a fantastic teacher—not just good, but fantastic. Students talk about you and your teaching. You want them to be positive and funnel their friends into your classes. You want a reputation for being a truly great instructor, not easy or hard. This book will help!

# Getting Ready to Teach

## Questions You Need to Ask

When you know where to go for help, where to hold office hours, and where to get copies, you can focus more on developing lessons to maximize student learning and less on wondering how to "do" and "get." Many new instructors don't even know the right questions to ask until they've been in the business awhile. To help make your life easier from the start, I have developed a comprehensive checklist that should include almost all the vital questions. Ask them. The answers will make your life easier!

Your official supervisor is frequently the Dean of Instruction or Vice President of Academics at a larger college, and a department chair at a smaller school. She or he may not be available very often, so ask your supervisor to recommend a faculty contact in your area who can answer all the mundane questions you'll have. This way you'll get acquainted right away with a faculty member and you won't be bothering your supervisor. Be sure to make friends with the department administrative assistants: They usually know everything and can be a tremendous help.

Supervisor's name: _____

   Home phone: _____

Faculty contact: _____

   Office phone: _____

   Home phone: _____

Dept. Administrative Assistant: _____

   Office phone: _____

College 800:_____

Emergency numbers to call if I can't make class: _____

Switchboard: _____

Weather station: _____

Pager or number for maintenance: _____

Pager or number for tech help: _____

My phone number at college: _____

My office at college: _____

College fax: _____

My e-mail here: _____

Room numbers and times for my classes: _____

_____

_____

_____

_____

_____

_____

_____

## *Checklist: Getting Ready*

❑ Faculty handbook for me? Faculty resources online?

❑ All pay and insurance paperwork filled out?

❑ In-service training I should or could attend?

❑ Faculty photo ID?

❑ Mailbox set up for me somewhere? When do I have access?

❑ Copy card or number? Access to copy room? Hours?

❑ Budget for copies?

❑ Computer to use? Printer? Scanner? Internet access?

❑ E-mail account set up? Who does this?

❑ Computer access codes? Programs available?
  Can I load test banks myself?

❑ Technology available in classrooms? Keys needed?

❑ Getting supplies—pens, overheads, etc.?

❑ Place arranged to meet students for office hours?

❑ Place to lock up my files? Materials?

❑ Access to an office area? When can I come in? Keys?

❑ Office hours policy for student contact?

❑ Textbook and ancillaries order? Who orders? Due date?

❑ Syllabus or example of common course outline?

❑ Campus teaching resource center services? Hours? Tour?

❑ Library services? Hours? Card? Tour?

❑ Policies, help, and information on student learning assessment?

❑ How to turn grades in? Midterm required?

❑ Any secretarial help available?

❑ Faculty evaluation process?

❑ Escort service for night classes? Number: _____

❑ Institutional core competencies to include in my course?

- ❑ Does program in which I teach have core competencies to include in my course?
- ❑ Emergency plan? Where?
- ❑ Policy for long-distance phone calls? Access codes?
- ❑ Date for decisions on hiring adjuncts next semester?
- ❑ Is there an on-line curriculum management system I can use? (Or am required to use?)
- ❑ Other issues: _____

# Course Design

## Goals and Objectives First

*A course is more than a textbook.*

Many of us associate a college course with "moving from chapter one to chapter fourteen"—or as close as we can get within the academic term. We allow the textbook to *become* the course design. With a perfect text, matched perfectly to your audience, this may be OK to begin with. And certainly, when you are hired a week before classes start, this is probably all you can do the first semester. But textbooks are developed for generalized needs, not your particular needs. Besides, you are the expert: Students expect more than just a reiteration of the text. After all, they can read the text on their own.

*Start by developing goals for your course. Ask yourself, "What broad topics/issues do my students need to know when they leave my course?"*

Will you be introducing students to seven modes of essay development? To procedures in QuickBooks? To basic statistical concepts? To the Bill of Rights?

*Goals are broad statements about what your course will cover or accomplish.*

Goals are frequently found in catalog course descriptions—but not always. Or, you can usually locate the goals other faculty in your department have developed in common course outlines or syllabi for your course. You should not set goals that diverge widely from the goals developed by others for the same course.

Your course likely fits into a program of study with expectations that students in the program are to acquire certain knowledge and skills all along. Find where your course fits into the overall program of study and how much leeway you have to add or subtract goals for your course.

Good textbooks outline their goals. Many of those goals will suit your needs. There is no need to reinvent the wheel when it is already round and rolling.

*Next, develop outcomes or objectives for your students. Ask yourself, "With what knowledge and abilities should my students leave my course?"*

Objectives are what the students leave knowing or are able to do.

For each of your course goals, you should set several objectives, in order to cover it well. Objectives provide evidence that you and your students have achieved each goal. If you have time, develop your own objectives for your course. It may help you to focus if you think of objectives as outcomes.

Again, objectives may be dictated by your department, so ask first. And again, good textbooks list objectives for every chapter's big goals. You can

use and modify some or all of the objectives in the textbook, but you should end up with objectives that relate directly to your course goals. Textbooks usually have way too many objectives for you to use them all.

*What are good objectives?*

• Good objectives relate directly to course goals.

• Good objectives are clear and specific.

*Example:* Students will be able to choose an appropriate phlebotomy technique for drawing blood, adapting to the health and presentation of veins.

When developing objectives, ask yourself, "In the context of the goals set for the course, what do my students need to know when they walk out the door?"

• What knowledge bites should they possess?
  *In an intro psych course, what should every student know by the end? Which big theories? Big names? Research findings on which topics?*

• What skills, procedures, and/or processes should they have developed?
  *Interpreting research data? Setting up a microscope? Critical thinking? Analyzing a research article? Inputting data into a statistical program?*

• What understandings should they have?
  *How parenting practices impact intelligence?*

• What attitudes should they demonstrate?
  *Healthy skepticism?*

If you check out a book on writing objectives, you'll find that K–12 student teachers are frequently taught to write objectives with three points: *Given a blank map* [condition]*, students will be able to identify the countries of Europe* [behavior] *with 80% accuracy* [criterion for assessing performance].

If you want to write objectives in this style, great, go for it! But, according to current research, this level of detail isn't really necessary. Instead, come up with a few basic, salient objectives for each goal, at the appropriate level for your course.

The trick? *You must be able to measure student success for each of your objectives.* If you have no way to really measure whether or not students have actually achieved the objective, then your objective is most likely too vague, too broad, or too lofty.

Make your objectives/outcomes realistic for the level of your course:

- An introductory course lays a foundation. It skims the surface. You don't need to teach or test on every concept in the field! What are the *big* ideas appropriate to the course level?

- Upper-division courses cover subjects in more depth. For these you need to find out what courses are prerequisites for yours and get their descriptions. This way you know what you can expect your students to have already learned and you can develop your objectives accordingly.

## Objectives and Bloom's Taxonomy

I frequently hear faculty members complain that students can't think. But what can they expect if they only ask them to memorize information and spit it back? You can do better than that—and Bloom's taxonomy can help.

Way back in 1956, Benjamin S. Bloom, then Associate Director of the Board of Examinations of the University of Chicago, wanted to develop a way to classify statements of instructional objectives. He assembled measurement specialists from across the United States and they developed a hierarchy of levels for instructional objectives, published as *Taxonomy of Educational Objectives: The Classification of Educational Goals*. Bloom's taxonomy consists of three domains: cognitive, affective, and psychomotor. For each they established a hierarchy of learning in terms of complexity.

It didn't take long for researchers and teachers to adopt the taxonomy as a guide to developing objectives. Bloom's taxonomy is critical to course design for every area from physics to modern dance. While some classes (such as counseling, theater, dance) may involve two or even all three domains, most college courses will involve primarily the cognitive domain—thinking—so we focus on only this domain here.

Memorization of knowledge is the lowest level of thinking. If you want a higher level of thinking, you have to ask different questions and assign different projects. In the table on the following page, you can see how useful the taxonomy is to planning.

Plan to move from the lower levels to higher levels, from perhaps the first paper (a factual report, for example) to the last paper (an evaluation). But plan for complexity within all tests and assignments. And remember that the lower levels are important prerequisites to the higher levels in any field. It is hard to synthesize and evaluate knowledge that you don't have!

Although the taxonomy is arranged in a hierarchy, it becomes obvious very quickly that knowledge is not so neatly compartmentalized. Most projects and tests at the college level should certainly involve multiple levels.

(If you are completely unfamiliar with Bloom's taxonomy, go to the Web and do a search. There are many good sites that will be of tremendous benefit to you, such as *eduscapes.com/tap/topic69.htm* and *enpubfulton.asu.edu/mcneill/blooms.htm.*)

In 2001, Lorin Anderson and David R. Krathwohl, two people who had worked with Bloom, published a revision of the taxonomy, developed by a group of educators (*A Taxonomy for Learning, Teaching and Assessing: A Revision of Bloom's Taxonomy of Educational Objectives*). The following is a summary of the revised taxonomy (pp. 67–68):

- **Remembering:** Retrieving, recognizing, and recalling relevant knowledge from long-term memory.

- **Understanding:** Constructing meaning from oral, written, and graphic messages through interpreting, exemplifying, classifying, summarizing, inferring, comparing, and explaining.

- **Applying:** Carrying out or using a procedure through executing or implementing.

- **Analyzing:** Breaking material into constituent parts, determining how the parts relate to one another and to an overall structure or purpose through differentiating, organizing, and attributing.

| Level in the Cognitive Domain | Explanation | Appropriate Objectives |
|---|---|---|
| Knowledge (lowest) | If your students have to remember it—facts, sequences, categories, theories, methods, criteria, etc.— they are functioning at the knowledge level. Don't underestimate this level— it is critical! | Student will be able to recognize or recall XYZ. Student will list the criteria for XYZ. Student will sequence the phases in XYZ. |
| Comprehension | This level requires translation, extrapolation, understanding. | Student will be able to summarize, illustrate, explain, or paraphrase XYZ. Student will define XYZ in his or her own words. |
| Application | This level involves using the material learned at the knowledge and comprehension levels, applying it to a problem or a new situation. | Student will be able to apply his or her knowledge of XYZ to solve the following problem… |
| Analysis | At this level, students should be taking things apart, recognizing patterns, analyzing relationships, seeing connections, finding major elements, dissecting, and recognizing relationships. | Student will be able to distinguish, classify, and relate assumptions about XYZ. |
| Synthesis | This is the creative level. Students combine, integrate, etc. to develop something new— pattern, piece, structure, theory. | Student will be able to integrate, combine ideas, develop new XYZ. |
| Evaluation (highest) | Students should be able to evaluate, judge, and justify using criteria. | Student will be able to appraise, assess, evaluate XYZ. |

- **Evaluating:** Making judgments based on criteria and standards through checking and critiquing.

- **Creating:** Putting elements together to form a coherent or functional whole; reorganizing elements into a new pattern or structure through generating, planning, or producing.

## Projects and Assignments and Bloom's Taxonomy

If you have the time when designing a course, use a planning table so you are sure to include all levels of Bloom's taxonomy for in-class activities and out-of-class assignments. You can easily see how this type of table helps an instructor think seriously about planning. Many people *think* they are teaching and assessing at the highest levels of thinking—until they write out all their objectives and activities and get shocked at how many of them are at the two lowest levels of Bloom. You can easily avoid this situation with a grid and some planning. (See English Composition examples on p. 18.)

If you are a spreadsheet or table fan, then you know the fun you can have getting this organized. You might want to add extra columns for the means you'll use to assess progress toward the objective (formative or summative), the materials you'll need for the lesson, etc. Once you have a plan, it's yours for good! (Well, at least until you improve it!)

## Textbooks and Ancillary Materials

### Textbooks
A good text is almost essential for a good undergraduate course—although it certainly is no *guarantee*.

You may not have a choice of books. Find out if the college wants you to use a specific textbook. What are other teachers using? The bookstore may have already purchased used books.

If you're free to choose, get free instructor copies of several texts to peruse. The bookstore or your faculty contact can tell you how to work through a book rep if you don't know how.

| Week | Basic Objective | Activity in Class | Assignment (out) | Bloom Level |
|---|---|---|---|---|
| 1 | Understand elements of Introductions | Identify parts in class (overhead with sample Introductions) | | Knowledge |
| | | Evaluate and rank three sample Introductions (in groups)— justify ranking | | Evaluation |
| | | | Write an intro with all the parts and label the parts | Understanding, application, and synthesis |
| 2 | Recognize concision in writing; be able to edit for concision | Identify wordy sentences with guidance on overhead (whole class) | | Understanding |
| | | | Eliminate wordiness from three paragraphs (provide the paragraphs; group work) | Analysis, application |

- Compare several texts if you have time, but *order on time.*

- Look for currency, clear writing, and appealing visual format (not just page after page of small print).

- Does the text match the emphasis and goals of your course?

- Are there objectives clearly detailed for each chapter?

- Are there multiple examples for concepts? Charts? Color? Tables? (Charts, graphs, histograms, photos, etc. help with difficult concepts.)

- Are key terms pulled out and defined for students?

- Are there review questions for each chapter?

- Is it the appropriate reading level? (Reading level can usually be checked officially in the campus teaching resource center.)

Consider *cost* to students. Some books are ghastly expensive, yet offer little more information than significantly less costly books. Is soft-cover available? Don't require multiple texts for a class if you plan on assigning only small parts of them. Students are very resentful (and rightly so) when this happens.

*Remember:* the text should not define the course. You can switch chapter order when you teach and skip some chapters, if necessary, as well as add material.

Your bookstore personnel are your friends—or your enemies. Order early and don't switch orders on them at the last minute! Don't order too many "recommended" texts per class; not all students will purchase them, which makes it difficult for the store to determine how many to order.

### Ancillary Materials
Every good textbook should have a full ancillary package. Find out about CD-ROMs, test banks, connected Web sites, PowerPoint presentations, videos, diagnostic tests, study guides, and—especially—instructor's guides with outlines, goals, and objectives.

A good instructor's guide frequently has objectives already aligned with Bloom's taxonomy for you. Check this out. (Good test banks are also keyed to Bloom.)

If the ancillaries you want aren't free, who pays for them? Find out before ordering. Who gets to keep them?

# Pacing and Variety

## Pacing

If you don't use a semester planning sheet, it's easy to get ahead of yourself and have nothing much to do the last two weeks ... or, worse, get behind and have to cram in too much at the end. Plan carefully to spread out the workload. Always have extra activities on hand in case the ones you use take half as much time as expected. But make sure those activities involve critical thinking and are meaningful. Students know when you are adding "busy work" to fill a poorly planned class!

All chapters are not created equal, even in the best textbooks, so if you are planning "one week = one chapter" you might get stung. Some chapters can be combined; others will take several days of activities to help students truly understand a difficult concept.

Don't schedule all major projects in your classes to be due on the same day or you'll have a hard time giving the students a fast turnaround and you'll go nuts correcting too much at once.

Don't assume that because you've covered it, they understand it. Use formative assessment techniques to check understanding and change your speed to adjust to the results. (More later on formative assessment.)

If you use small groups for your in-class activities, get ready for "group speed disparity." You will find some groups zoom through the activity and others dawdle along. Those dawdlers might just be thinking harder—or else they are way off target and socializing instead of working. When you use small group activities, walk around the class and join each group multiple times so you can help students pace themselves. Also, have an extension of the assignment ready to pass out to the speediest groups, to keep them working rather than discussing the weekend.

## Variety: Learning Styles

There's a lot of research, pro and con, on the topic of learning styles. Proponents say students have a certain preferred learning style (visual, auditory, or kinesthetic) and learn best when information is presented in that style. Skeptics say research doesn't reveal any big learning differences to support that position on learning styles.

We say this: plan ahead to use visual, auditory, and kinesthetic variety in your lectures, in your in-class activities, and in the projects and assignments you'll use to assess your students. That way you are fully covered. This is basically sound teaching!

Important: it is *not* considered "variety" to stand and talk (auditory) about a PowerPoint (visual) while students take notes (kinesthetic)!!! Too much of this can be a huge bore!

# *Checklist: Course Design*

- ❑ Check with the department first about any goals required for your course(s).
- ❑ Check to see if any objectives are required or assumed.
- ❑ Check to see if any text is required, preferred, or already ordered.
- ❑ Develop a few broad goals appropriate to the course level.
- ❑ Select the textbook carefully to match your goals.
- ❑ Order the ancillaries. (First find out who pays.)
- ❑ Develop specific objectives for each of your goals.
- ❑ When writing objectives, take into consideration the knowledge, skills, procedures, processes, understandings, and attitudes with which students need to leave your class.
- ❑ Use a planning sheet to chart your presentation of objectives for the term.
- ❑ Design assignments that correlate directly to your objectives.
- ❑ Make sure that no assignment could be viewed as busy work, and that all assignments are worth the time you expect the students to invest in them.
- ❑ Plan a wide variety of ways to teach, involving visual, auditory, and kinesthetic modes.
- ❑ Consider *pacing* of reading load and assignments. Allow students enough time to do a good job on projects. Allow yourself enough time to prepare and to grade projects.
- ❑ Spread major points/projects throughout the term, to avoid overloading the students toward the end.
- ❑ Plan some type of assessment for all objectives so you know students have learned what you intend them to learn.
- ❑ Plan time for formative assessment. (More on this later.)
- ❑ Plan activities, projects, and assessments across all levels of Bloom's taxonomy.

# Course Management

## Syllabus

I can't stand wimpy little one-page syllabi that give so little information about a class that it is basically a waste of paper. When preparing a syllabus, more is better. If you work as an adjunct, you frequently are harder to contact than "regular" instructors, so you need to be ultra clear in your syllabi and provide plenty of contact info.

A good syllabus should include the following:
- an overview of the course
- class location and time
- instructor contact info
- required texts and materials
- course goals
- objectives
- list of assignments
- grading scale
- attendance policies
- teaching methods

A schedule of assignments with due dates as well as any grading rubrics should be attached.

(You may be unfamiliar with the term *rubric*. It's basically a simplified way to grade a complicated assignment or test. It's a list of criteria, "the things that count," with some indication of levels of quality for each criterion.)

The sample syllabus below shows each of these sections (with comments in parentheses and additional ideas in blocks).

---

### *English 101—Introduction to Composition (3 credits)*

**Overview of this course:**
Introduction to Composition is a basic college writing course exploring the different modes of development used in typical college coursework, such as narrative, process writing, cause-and-effect, and persuasion. In addition, this course covers writing and researching for the basic academic research paper.

**Class time and place:**
Tuesday/Thursdays 1:00-2:45 in Armstrong Hall 345

**Your Instructor:** Dr. Patricia Linehan

**Office Phone:** XXX-XXXX   **Home Phone:** XXX-XXXX   *(If you want to include it)*

**Office:** E121   **Office Hours:** TWH, 1:00-3:00

**E-mail:** XXXX@XXXXXXXXX.XXX

**Required textbooks and materials:**
*(List texts and any other materials, such as a computer diskette, spiral notebook, etc.)*

**Broad course goals:**
1. Introduce writing as a process of prewriting, drafting, revision.

2. Give students experience with seven modes of development.

3. Provide tools and opportunities for academic research.

4. Etc.

## Objectives:
Students will be able to:

1. Identify and use seven modes of development.

2. Tailor writing for specific audiences.

3. Proofread their work and correct errors.

4. Etc.

 *These objectives are important, because they give you a "script" for planning your lessons. To ensure that students will be able to do these things by the end of the course, you have to set up the right types of learning situations and use the right methods to assess their progress.*

*Students love knowing exactly what they will get out of a course, but not every instructor includes all objectives in a syllabus. If you do not want to include all objectives, you might choose to list "sample objectives" for each goal. But at some point you do need to let students know all the objectives for the course, so why not here?*

## Basis of grade:

| You will be graded on the following: | % of grade | Points |
|---|---|---|
| Five five-paragraph essays: | 50% | 40 each |
| One 10-page research paper: | 30% | 120 |
| In-class activities: | 20% | 80 |

**Total points for semester:** 400

It is useful to check the workload assigned by others teaching the same class. You may want to have a similar number of assignments.

Avoid creating a situation in which a student could amass enough "in-class" points to get a good grade despite dismal test or project grades. If you give "in-class" points, give them only for a real activity you grade or for documented contributions to discussions, not just for attendance. Make "in-class" activity points available on random days, to encourage attendance. Students should not get a grade for "being there"—attendance is a "given."

If you tend to "flex" midstream and alter assignments, I recommend not telling how many points each assignment is worth here: this gives you flexibility later. Decide on a total number of points for the course—fairly arbitrary—and tell students the percentage each component will be of the total.

If you choose not to give point totals for each graded assignment, it's easy to work out a system for converting total points in each category to a percentage of the final grade. Your college may require use of an on-line curriculum or course management system which easily does the calculation for you.

**Grading scale:**

93-100% . . . . A

86-92%. . . . . . B

80-85% . . . . . C

75-80% . . . . . D

Below 75. . . . . F

The college may have a set grading scale. If so, you'll need to use it. Many faculty use 90-100% = A, 80-89% = B, etc. Others feel this is too easy. Does the department have a preference?)

**Missed class and late assignment policies:**
Attendance is expected. If we are going to become a "learning community," then we all have to be here! In-class activities cannot be made up without a doctor or military excuse. Because I know "life happens," I will drop the two lowest scores from each student's in-class activities when I compute grades. I will accept late assignments for full points with a doctor or military excuse if turned in within one week of due date. I will dock other late assignments one-half grade per week. I will take into consideration extenuating circumstances on a case-by-case basis.

**Teaching methods for this class:**
Lecture . . . . . . . . . . . . . . . 20%
Peer editing and sharing . . . 15%
Media (videos, etc.) . . . . . . . . 5%
In-class Activities . . . . . . . . 30%
On computers, writing . . . . 30%

Think ahead very carefully if you choose to give a point total for all assignments within the syllabus, rather than just percentages of the total grade. How much should in-class activities be worth each day? If you choose 10 points, then 16 weeks X 10 points equals 160 points. If this equals 20% of the grade, how many hundreds of points are you calculating for projects and tests? You can end up working with huge numbers.

## Schedule Table

Make a table of all assignments on a separate page and staple it to the syllabus (see example on p. 28). Students will then know what they are responsible for every day, all semester. This cuts out a lot of unnecessary e-mail ("What's due tomorrow?") and excuses ("I didn't know we were supposed to turn that in today.")

| Class | Attendance Signature | Due the Day of Class | Points Available | Points Earned |
|---|---|---|---|---|
| 1/12 | | Introduction | | |
| | | Diagnostic tests | | |
| 1/26 | | Chapters 1, 2 | | |
| | | Quiz | 10 | |
| | | Reading: King p. 506 | | |
| | | In-Class Activity | 5 | |
| 2/2 | | Chapters 3, 4 | | |
| | | Quiz | 10 | |
| | | Reading: Asfahani p. 502 | | |
| | | In-Class Activity | 5 | |
| | | **First Essay: Description** | 50 | |
| 2/9 | | Chapters 5, 6 | | |
| | | Quiz | 10 | |
| | | Reading: Haubegger p. 500 | | |
| | | In-Class Activity | 5 | |
| 2/23 | | Chapter 9 | | |
| | | Quiz | 10 | |
| | | Reading: Morales p. 498 | | |
| | | In-Class Activity | 5 | |
| | | **Second Essay: Process** | 50 | |
| 3/1 | | Chapter 14 | | |
| | | Quiz | 10 | |
| | | Reading: Angelou p. 464 | | |
| | | In-Class Activity | 5 | |
| 3/15 | | Chapter 7 | | |
| | | Quiz | 10 | |
| | | Reading: Mabry p. 466 | | |

# Student Contact/Contract Sheet

You need a way to contact your students in case you have to suddenly cancel a class, or to contact a student who is missing a vital assignment before you turn in final grades. I suggest that on the first day you have students fill out a contact/contract sheet. Keep it in a locked filing cabinet because student phone numbers are private information. I also suggest you ask for more than a phone number. Ask questions that will help you tailor your class demonstrations, activities, and examples, and help you *build up the value* of your subject area for students. Also have students sign a statement that says they have read and understand the syllabus.

---

### Contact/Contract Sheet
### for English Composition Section 60

Name: _____

E-mail: _____

Phone for emergency contact
if class needs to be cancelled: _____

My top three goals for this course:

1. _____

   _____

2. _____

   _____

3. _____

   _____

Major: _____ Minor: _____

Two questions I have about this subject area:

1. _____

_____

2. _____

_____

Other courses I have taken in this subject: _____

_____

_____

Interests, hobbies, or goals I have that material in this course might touch upon:

Example: ~~I love to garden and I hate bugs but I hate using chemical~~ sprays even more. I'm hoping this entomology class will teach me some alternative for dealing with insects.

_____

_____

_____

I have read and understand the syllabus: (Please sign below.)

_____

# Organization: Class-in-a-Box

Organization and "no surprises" are the keys to good college level course management. When you are disorganized or students get surprised by new assignments, point changes, etc., they can get easily disgruntled. For organization, I have used the *class-in-a-box* system for years and made many converts among full-time and adjunct faculty for this technique.

It is particularly useful for adjunct faculty who have to remain "portable" and sometimes do not have a desk area. Even if you are teaching four different courses at four colleges, the class-in-a-box system will keep you highly organized. No more lost papers—and better teacher/student communication!

Introduce this system on day one and remind students about *returning their folders at the end of every class* for a couple more weeks. Truly, this is a *great system*!

The basics:

❑ A plastic box with a carrying handle for each class

❑ Hanging files that hold syllabi, overheads, pens, dry-erase markers, tests, keys, roll lists, etc.

❑ One file folder labeled for each student (in various colors, so students can find theirs quickly)

Here's how it works:

1. Staple a duplicate of your syllabus schedule into each folder, with all assignments and the points available for each one and a place for students to sign each day they attend. (For federal financial aid purposes, you may have to report the last day of class attendance. This way you will have a clear record.)

2. At the beginning of the class, each student picks up his or her folder. At the end, they stack them next to the box. You can quickly mark the unclaimed folders "absent."

3. Set penalties for taking a folder from the classroom, such as major point deductions. For a few weeks, remind students to return their folders, to develop the habit.

4. Students turn in papers and other assignments by putting them into their folders.

5. Use the syllabus schedule sheet to write notes to your students: use a red pen for "see me" comments and a green pen for "fine." Explain your system on the first day of class and the students should quickly learn to glance at the sheet for comments and respond.

6. Return all papers and assignments to your students by putting them into their folders. This keeps grades and any marginal comments private, which students appreciate.

7. Have students take home what you've graded and recorded.

8. When you grade assignments, write the points earned in the folders. Students will always know the status of their grades.

*Note:* Also record the grades in a grade book or on-line course manager, in case a student leaves with his or her folder and loses it.

## No Surprises = Satisfaction

Students are happiest when they know what they are going to learn, how the class will run, exactly what is expected of them, how assignments will be graded, how you are going to teach and communicate with them, and when everything is due. They hate it when instructors add assignments during the term, rather than plan everything out ahead of time. When they know all requirements in advance, they can really decide whether they want to commit to your class that first day. This is important. They know the workload and sign on for the ride. The result is informed students who won't gripe and who will be more satisfied throughout the term.

# Checklist: Course Management

❏ Locate sample syllabi or a common course outline for the courses you are teaching.

❏ Develop a class-in-a-box organization system or something else that will work to handle paper flow.

❏ Create a detailed syllabus for each course.

❏ Pass out the syllabus and discuss it well on the first day of class.

❏ Put extra copies in each file box. (Students lose them or add the course late. Be ready.)

❏ Plan carefully so you can stick to the syllabus and won't need to change it.

❏ Post your syllabus to the college's on-line curriculum or course management system.

In the syllabus:

❏ Include a general description of the course (see the college catalog) to create interest.

❏ Include general goals for the course to create more interest.

❏ Include specific objectives that tell the students what they will learn in class. Check the textbook for good ones. Don't get *too* detailed or you'll overwhelm your students.

❏ Include a list of all graded assignments, due dates, and points each is worth.

❏ Include an explanation of grading scales.

❏ Include a class-by-class schedule table. Check the college calendar for days off before designing it or you'll end up revising.

❏ Include your office location, phone numbers, and office hours.

❏ Include your attendance policy and information on make-up or late assignments.

❏ Include the basics of how you teach and/or structure the class.

❑ Attach any grading rubrics that are appropriate. (See the next chapter, "Grading Issues." It's good to pass out rubrics with the syllabus, if possible.)

❑ Include a contact/contract sheet, including the statement "I have read and understand this syllabus" for students to sign, that you can file in a locked cabinet.

❑ Include a statement for students with disabilities about any alternative formats available (such as Braille, large print, and cassette tapes) and/or services available through the campus teaching resources center or the writing center. (Many colleges require such statements in each syllabus.)

# Grading Issues

## Scales

Be sure to check if your college recommends or requires a specific grading scale. If not, check with other instructors to see if there is an unofficial grading scale agreement among them. You do not want to set your scale vastly higher or lower than other faculty. Remember: a few points make a big difference to students.

Think about your scale: Should a student still pass a course if he or she knows only 60% of the material? (Would you want that engineer to design a bridge you drive over?)

## Privacy

You cannot post grades on your office door or outside your classroom using student names, even just their last names, their Social Security numbers, or their student IDs. Also, you cannot pass a list of grades around class with any of the above information on it.

Here's a solution to the privacy problem. Write numbers from 1 to the total of students on small round adhesive labels. Cut the labels up individually and pass them around class. Have each student take a label and stick it inside his or her folder in a certain place. You can then use their numbers in your grade book and post grades anywhere with these numbers, legally.

If a parent calls and wants to know how his or her student is doing, you cannot reveal any information if the student is over 18, unless the student has signed a special waiver.

Do not give papers or grades to anyone besides the student—not friends, not roommates, not anyone.

## Fairness in Grading

You must be fair with grades. If you let any student make up a quiz for any reason, you'll need to make that quiz available for all students for equivalent reasons. Then you get in the messy area of deciding what constitutes a worthy excuse. ("How many times has your grandmother died?") I recommend dropping the lowest two or three quiz scores and not allowing make-ups except for doctor or military excuses. This spares you a lot of uncomfortable decision-making.

The halo effect is a fact of life. We are human. We cannot avoid wanting some students to do well because they're so nice, for example, and wanting others to do less well, because they don't seem to pay attention in class.

You need to control for the halo effect. Have students write their numbers, not their names, on the back of all papers, so you grade each paper without knowing which student submitted it.

Do not always collect essay tests in the same order. Have written criteria for right answers. Don't grade essays all at once in a marathon session or when you are already exhausted. The first and last essays will likely get a different reading if you do.

Strive to design as many projects/tests as possible that you can grade objectively. This way your feelings won't be a liability.

Set the criteria for grades in the grading/evaluation section of your syllabus and stick to your plan.

Avoid the impression of subjective grading on your more "subjective" projects by using a good, sound, grading rubric that breaks down the key grading criteria fully for students. Give this rubric to students as they are preparing their papers or projects; don't keep grading rubrics secret.

Keep good records. Believe me, at some point you'll have to justify a grade.

## Grade Inflation

How do you want to be known as a teacher—as the "easy A"? Probably not. But creeping grade inflation, especially in courses with subjective projects, is sometimes a problem. You want to be known as fair, not easy, so be sure to set your standards high enough to differentiate between students who really do know the material at the "A level" and those who do not.

Should you adopt a bell curve in your grading? I do not suggest this. *If you are doing good active teaching and giving your students multiple opportunities to work with the content and to overlearn, most of your students should not be earning C's. But also it is rare in an undergraduate class for most students to earn A's. If your grades are too loaded with A's and B's and you have very few C's and D's, look at your standards and graded assignments. Are you offering too many easy point opportunities that don't really reflect college-level work and don't really discriminate between those who put forth the effort to study and understand the material and those who don't? When a student earns an F, assign it. Students *earn* grades; you don't give them.

## How Do You Grade Participation?

Grading discussion is challenging. You will want to experiment. Giving points for participation can be contentious, because if you don't track which student is talking at the time he or she is talking, you are grading later on general impressions—and memory, frankly, isn't that accurate and is influenced by the halo effect. Some instructors mark down each time a student participates on a check sheet, but you have to know your students' names well, of course, and marking contributions can be time-consuming.

One instructor we knew gave each student sticks with his or her name on them at the beginning of each class and then collected them as students made worthwhile comments. Some of her students complained it was "babyish," but it actually worked well to get more students talking to earn points.

When giving participation points, you must come up with an objective way to calculate them—and explain your method in the syllabus.

If you give points for in-class activities, use criteria. Don't give full points for "doing" the activity. There should be a point difference between barely participating and actively jumping in, asking challenging questions, and discussing fully.

# Checklist: Grading Issues

❑ Check for a college-wide grading scale you have to use.

❑ Is there an unofficial grading scale to consider?

❑ Structure your points so students who really don't have an "A's worth" of knowledge can't get an A in the course.

❑ Think deeply about the nature of your subject area and how important it is to this student and the people depending upon this student's skills in the future. Develop your grading scale accordingly. For example, in a course for medical lab technicians on typing blood, should a student be able to pass if accurate only 70% of the time? 80%? 90%? At 90% accuracy a student is likely to kill one in 10 patients by mislabeling blood. Some classes must work at the mastery level: students must master the material to pass. Many college classes are not of this nature (history, English, philosophy, sales, marketing), but you need to think about this issue if your own courses contain *vital* skills or knowledge.

❑ Develop a system to communicate grades with students while at the same time protecting their privacy.

❑ Develop a policy for making up quizzes, classes, tests, and assignments that can be fair to all students and allow some "life events" to happen to them without destroying their grade.

❑ Plan for as many objectively graded projects and tests as possible.

❑ Place all important grading issues in the syllabus.

❑ Develop good grading rubrics for the projects and papers ahead of time and attach them to the syllabus.

❑ Develop a good grade book system for each class, one that is easy to keep and yet incorporates all the details for the term.

❑ Establish a way to effectively give points for participating in discussions.

❑ Develop (and include in the syllabus) a small rubric for in-class activity points.

*Assessment*

## Major Issues and Definitions

Documentation of the assessment of student learning has taken on new emphasis in the last decade, partially fueled by requirements from college accreditation bodies, partially fueled by a new demand for accountability within American culture at large. College instructors need to be able to show what students have actually learned by taking their course or program.

This is a hot topic in higher education as student assessment continues to expand way beyond end-of-term final exam grades. I can only give you an overview here and suggest you check the resource list for additional reading on assessment.

### The True Purpose of Assessment

The true purpose of assessment is meaningful change that positively impacts student learning, not giving students a grade. For example, if I know students are consistently misunderstanding the concept of classical conditioning because I assessed their understanding after my presentation and they failed, then I know I need to change something in my method of teaching this concept. Do I need better examples? Do students need a different set of activities? Why aren't they getting it? Good assessment, timed well, drives changes in instruction and curriculum development to benefit student learning. It is *not* just evaluation at the end of a semester. Good assessment is an early-warning system, a guidance system, and an evaluation system.

## Institutional and Departmental Plans and Programs

Your college should have a formal, written assessment program. In addition, your department or program will also have a formal assessment plan, which is important for you to locate. You want to be part of the team approach to assessing student outcomes; if all the other English or machine tool or electronics instructors are using a common rubric for papers, projects, or other assignments, you should explore using the same one.

## Formative Assessment: Your "Early-Warning" Guidance System

Formative assessment is ongoing throughout the term and is not connected to grading. These assessment efforts tell you what and how much your students understand, so you can adjust your teaching, projects, and activities *right now* so they will hopefully understand more and better.

### Summative Assessment: Evaluating Student Outcomes

This is the type of assessment all instructors are familiar with: evaluation—the grade. It generally comes at the end of the term, but parts can come throughout the course. This is "high stakes" assessment and students want it fair, clear, and highly connected to the course objectives.

This type of assessment is also a guidance system for instructors who want to improve their course. When a lot of students fail to demonstrate knowledge or skill in an area during summative assessment, then instructors know they need to change something—maybe the textbook, maybe how they present topics, how they develop activities to help students understand concepts, or how they test. The results of summative assessment should inform course design.

### Direct and Indirect Measures

It is important to understand the difference between *direct* and *indirect* assessment measures.

**Direct measures** actually measure student learning outcomes directly. There are many possibilities for both formative and summative assessment. A direct measure could be a final paper graded on a rubric—a project that demonstrates achievement of one essential objective—or a verbal presentation explaining the relationship between two concepts. With direct measures, a student must demonstrate skill, knowledge, or understanding.

Programs should have direct measures in place (such as capstone projects or courses) to test skills and knowledge before graduation. Course-level assessments should certainly be keyed in to the types of program assessments in place and help students work toward mastering the necessary components of those capstone assessments. (Examples are shown on p. 43.)

**Indirect measures** do not result in the same kind of "show me what you know" assessments. Indirect measures can only *infer* skill, knowledge, and/or understanding. Surveys asking students how much they learned, surveys asking employers if graduates know such-and-such, graduation rates, employment rates, student satisfaction inventories—all these are indirect measures. They are not direct proof of student learning, but they do give the institution information which might help instructors re-vision teaching techniques, curriculum, and program offerings.

| Program-Level Direct Assessment | Course-Level Direct Assessment |
|---|---|
| **Case Study:** Develop a marketing program for a global firm | **Test:** over elements of a marketing plan<br>**Paper:** on considerations for global marketing |
| **Project:** Develop a construction management plan for a 75-unit apartment complex in St. Paul, MN | **Test:** over project management<br>**Paper:** over legal/permit considerations<br>**Project:** case study on hiring subcontractors |
| PRAXIS (teacher certification exam) | Test/papers/demonstrations of knowledge on objectives specific to the PRAXIS |

At the course level, good assessment should focus primarily on direct measures, not indirect measures. Although we all like to know if students enjoy our courses, enjoyment is not the essential target outcome because enjoyment does not equate to knowledge, understanding, or skills.

However, I also suggest you ask students for feedback at several points during the term about how the class is going for them and how you can improve the learning environment. This is extremely important information and will help you craft the best learning situations.

## Direct Measures of Student Learning

### Formative Direct Measures

Remember: formative assessment takes place throughout the term and is your early-warning system about what is going right and what is going wrong. Because you will be using formative techniques a lot, you need various techniques or you will bore your students. Variety is helpful, not only to add "spice" to formative assessment, but also to enable you to look at student learning from many angles. This helps you find out what is really going on.

There are several good books out on formative assessment techniques, commonly referred to as "CATs" (classroom assessment techniques). I suggest you purchase any book by Thomas A. Angelo and K. Patricia Cross, who have written extensively and clearly on this topic. Your faculty development library probably has copies of the Angelo and Cross books for checkout, but these books are worth owning.

On day one, introduce the concept of CATs to your class. Tell them that formative assessment is your "finger on the pulse" of student understanding—and you use CATs only to help you become a better instructor and to find those areas you need to explain again. Once students realize you are not going to grade these assessments, that they don't take much time, and that you will actually use them to find out what you need to explain again or refashion, they are very willing participants. However, if you keep doing CATs and never change anything, you lose their goodwill.

Formative techniques embody the spirit of creativity and research—you are a detective trying to find out if students understand something, without threatening them via grades. With this mission, you can invent techniques appropriate to your subject material, students, and style.

There is nothing at all mysterious about this. The techniques I discuss on the next few pages include modifications of suggestions by Angelo and Cross and many other instructors who have developed and shared ideas. I suspect that all these techniques are being used by college instructors around the world, in one form or another, whether or not they ever read a book on classroom assessment techniques. Some CATs I've tried work better one term than another, but all have been good ways of gathering feedback. Experiment! Correlate your CATs to your objectives!

## Examples of Formative Direct Measures
### Classic Journalist's Summary
Angelo and Cross call this CAT the One-Sentence Summary, but for some concepts you might have to stretch it to the Two-Sentence Summary. It basically asks students to use an expanded set of classic journalism ques-

tions, the five W's and an H: who? what? when? where? how? why? You give students the topic (a concept, not a fact) and the prompts; they write the summary sentence(s).

I usually type this CAT up on a half sheet of paper. I ask for a few students (volunteers only) to share their responses in class; then all students place their summaries in a basket. I do not have students put these formative assessments into their folders because I don't grade them. I read all the responses and thereby gauge how well the students understand the concept and I can make adjustments in teaching it if necessary. This is a very effective technique and students like it—it stretches them.

---

**Journalist's Summary**
In one or two sentences *only*, answer the questions about the topic—Operant Conditioning

**Who? What? When? Where? How? Why?**

---

You could customize the direction and order of this example to check understanding for different levels of Bloom's taxonomy:

---

**Who "invented" it?** (knowledge-level answers)
**When?**
**What is it?**
**Who "uses" it?** (understanding and application answers)
**What is it used for?**
**When is it appropriate?** (evaluation)

---

**Theory into Practice**
This is a very simple technique, but it is good for assessing higher-order thinking skills at the application level. I introduce this technique verbally, go through an example on the board, and then give the students a half sheet of paper with only a few words to remind them of what to do. If stu-

dents cannot think of how the theory or concept you give them can be applied in "real life," then they probably do not understand it. You can narrow the parameters to fit your objectives, of course: "How could this be applied in geriatric nursing?" "How is this applied in the elementary math classroom?" "How is this applied during operant conditioning?"

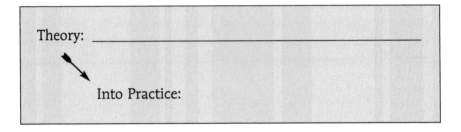

Theory: _____

          Into Practice:

### What's Still Confusing?

Whether you call this technique "The Muddiest Point" (Angelo and Cross) or find your own clever name relevant to your field (such as "Black Hole for Today" in astronomy), this is about as direct as it gets when asking for feedback. If you use it at the end of a class, you'll get several areas of concern because you will have covered numerous points. If you use it halfway through, responses will be more targeted. If you use it right after introducing a complex topic, all responses will most likely focus on that one idea. Sometimes you get a lot of "nothing confusing—understood." This indicates success!

### Connections to the Past

When students link new information to old information, they are more likely to remember it. This technique works well when you have connected new material to material previously covered and want to make sure the students understand it. Again, the beauty of formative assessment is in its simplicity and the ease with which you can glance over the sheets for a holistic peek at how the whole class is doing. You decide how detailed you want students to get and can establish the criteria within your instructions.

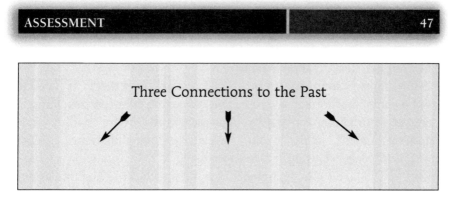

Three Connections to the Past

## Aha!

I find students really like this opportunity to talk briefly about an insight they had—an "aha moment," a sudden flash of understanding. This is not a formative assessment to use every day, because—let's face it—even in the best of classes, not every day has an "aha" in it. But watch your class and keep your half-sheets ready. When you see "light  bulbs" coming on, you might want to capture a better understanding of what happened with an "Aha!" sheet. This gives you clues as to which of your examples connect with students and will give you additional stories as your students explain their own "aha." Monitor responses for clarity of understanding.

## Draw and Label

In some subject areas you can tell at a glance if a concept is clear through the use of drawings or diagrams. In teaching educational psychology, I have students draw and label various concepts: conceptual hierarchies, classical conditioning of a child to math anxiety, a pod classroom arrangement to minimize the potential for running. If understanding a flow chart is important, you can provide the blank flow chart elements and have students label them.

Draw _____ and Label the essentials!

### The Defense Rests (Summarizing)

Having students summarize a process, a concept, or a theory is a good, solid technique of formative assessment. Of course, they do this without notes, so information is strictly in their own words. I have tried this as a "closing argument," to give it a little "sizzle," depending upon the concept. Examples: "Make a closing argument for using active learning in the classroom," and "Make a closing argument for the presence of groupthink during the Bay of Pigs." If the idea of a "closing argument" doesn't fit your topic, just ask for a summary!

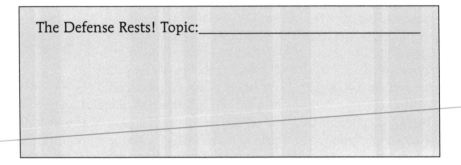

The Defense Rests! Topic:_____

## *Summative Direct Measures*

At some point, of course, you must assign grades. Then you are in the area of summative direct measures. You should set extremely clear criteria for projects, papers, portfolios, and presentations—in writing. Students need to know exactly which outcomes they are responsible for showing mastery of, and be able to have the grading rubric in hand while preparing so they know up front how you will judge their expertise.

### Most Frequently Used Summative Techniques

Use more than one of these!

*Comprehensive Final Exams*

    Make sure you provide good review opportunities and study guides listing the big ideas/concepts the test will cover.

*Portfolios*

    Have each student choose samples of his or her work from across the term.

*Final Projects*

As a summative assessment, a final project must incorporate several major objectives of the course. Example: a three-dimensional mockup of an office waiting room, fully decorated, for an interior design class.

*Final Papers*

As a summative assessment, a final paper should incorporate several major objectives of the class. It cannot be over just anything the student wants to discuss; you need to provide parameters.

*Culminating Presentations*

Again, the same concept: a culminating presentation should cover several major objectives.

*Oral Exams*

This used to be a favorite, one-on-one with the instructor. Several standard questions would prompt the student to sum up a lot of information from major objectives. Oral exams cause anxiety and much studying. They're extremely useful—and there's no cheating!

## Effective Tests and Use of Test Banks

- Test frequently—over each chapter, if possible, or once every two weeks. With smaller chunks to remember, students will learn more and be less anxious about testing. Midterms and finals as the sole tests are simply unacceptable. Give a comprehensive final exam, pulling from your chapter tests.

- Good textbooks come with test banks—usually in both paper and electronic formats. Choose a book with an appropriate test bank.

- Evaluate the test bank carefully. Some test banks are too difficult and "tricky." Others ask only knowledge questions at the "memorize these facts" level. The idea is to evaluate student learning in important areas in a field of study, not on trivia specific to one textbook.

- If the test bank consists of multiple-choice questions, how many distractors do questions have? Five distracters make multiple-choice questions quite a bit harder.

- Never select test bank items at random when making a test. Select items carefully to match your objectives.

- It is easier to go through the paper test bank and mark items that correlate with your objectives and then select them by number in your software package.

- Give adequate time to students taking tests. Some read slowly.

- Do not alter the chronological sequence of material, if possible. Keep the order in which it was presented in the book.

- Give students choices among multiple choice, essay, short answer, etc.

- I suggest putting a few "extra" items on each test, allowing students to choose 25 of 30 or 40 of 45. This actually relaxes students a great deal, as they feel slightly more in control of the situation. Instructors frequently use this option with essay items ("Choose two of the above five questions...") but somehow forget they can do this with other formats just as easily. It works well.

## Developing Your Own Test Items

Are you a glutton for punishment? Develop your own tests!

Test banks are an incredible help. After all, they are usually developed by subject area experts, they have more items than you could ever sanely use, and the publishers have usually performed item analysis to ascertain which items are "hard" and which are "easy." And let's face facts: all their essay items already have answers that you can make into handy checklists for grading. Test banks have a lot going for them!

Still, many instructors want to develop their own tests. Fine. Go to books or to the Web for the many resources that can tell you how to create good items. Many fine instructors create really bad multiple-choice or essay items! Here I am just raising some issues and offering some tips.

First and most important, don't use all one type of question item! Design items for all levels of Bloom!

## True/False

- First, ask yourself if it's worth developing true/false items. Will they really test student knowledge? Will they cover enough information? Will the results tell you what students know? Can you get enough depth into them? (Hard to do!)

- Make sure you cover major points, not insignificant items.

- Don't be tricky. What's the agenda here? Also, don't use negatives or double negatives. They make items harder to understand.

- Have students convert all false statements into true statements in order to get points. This helps eliminate the guessing, which is so easy with true/false items.

## Matching

- Ask yourself if matching items are worthwhile. Is simple recognition enough for you? A 10-point matching quiz at the beginning of each class session can sure help ensure that students read, and matching items aren't hard to make up! You can make this harder by having extra items on one side or the other.

- Most people use knowledge-level items for matching tests, but you can use scenarios that boost the level to understanding or application.

- Finally, for developing matching tests, Microsoft Word tables work great.

## Essays

- First of all, if you're only looking for facts, use a different test form. Essay tests are best when you want evaluation, synthesis, analysis, and/or application—all levels of thinking based upon knowledge and understanding.

- Create your answers as you create your test items. If the answers are not straightforward or become long and convoluted, then your essay item has multiple interpretations. Reword for clarity or avoid!

- If students are going to write by hand, try out your essay items yourself, by hand, to see how long your test takes. Then add a lot of extra minutes.

- Give a choice of essay items—but make sure each item is at the same level of difficulty.

- Essays cover less knowledge. Combine them with other test item types to make sure you test your students over a wide range of knowledge.

- Try "mini" essays—a cross between the essay and the "long" short answer.

- Teach your students how you want them to answer an essay item before you use any on a test. Do you want them to structure their essays with an intro, a body, and a conclusion? Don't assume they've learned this in high school.

- Decide if spelling and grammar are going to count and tell your students ahead of time. If an answer is correct but absolutely horribly written, how many points do you take off? Obviously, this will vary with subject area, but it bears consideration.

### Multiple-Choice

- Use the test bank. I've seen so many bad multiple-choice items that I do not suggest developing your own. If you insist, there are whole books written on this topic. Consult one!

- I know you're busy and you don't feel like searching for a book. Then at least read *How to Prepare Better Multiple-Choice Test Items: Guidelines for University Faculty*, by Steven J. Burton, Richard R. Sudweeks, Paul F. Merrill, and Bud Wood, attesting.byu.edu/info/handbooks/betteritems.pdf.

## Grading Rubrics: Formative and Summative Tools

When you are performing summative assessment that involves more than a true/false, matching, short answer, or multiple-choice item, you must have a scoring scheme to judge the quality of work. Instructors always have such a guide in their heads, but assessment accountability and good educational principles demand that you also have it on paper.

But rubrics aren't just for summative assessment. You can use them first in a formative manner (no grading)—and get a clear picture of students' "weaknesses" and "strengths" at any point in a project or paper. A "final" rubric first used on a draft paper gives students real guidance for revision. Rubrics are a great learning tool.

Rubrics seem so easy to develop—which means they are easy to develop badly! A good rubric takes some time and lots of serious thought, but once you've developed a good rubric, you can usually use it time and time again with only minor revisions.

Good rubrics:

- Focus on the major outcomes of the project being graded.
  - You must be able to identify the essence, the components of each outcome in detail. These are your criteria for grading.
  - The components or criteria you identify should be equal in importance, or weighted on the rubric.
- Use the professional language of your field.
- Have clear components or criteria; nothing is fuzzy or ambiguous.
- Have enough categories to differentiate among the levels of quality.
  - If you have too many (e.g., Bad, Poor, Average -, Average, Good, Good +, Excellent), you are making arbitrary decisions about quality.
  - If you have too few (e.g., Poor, Average, Terrific), the categories don't make sense or there are huge leaps in quality.
- Have a description for each quality category.
  - These tell your students what you expect of an A paper, a B paper, etc.
  - These provide a means of increasing reliability. Two graders looking at the same essay, paper, presentation, or portfolio should be able to come up with the same grade if the descriptions are clearly written. Without a description for each quality category, this is highly unlikely to happen. What is a "2" performance on a typical 1-4 scale? It doesn't mean the same to all graders if there's no clear description of "2"!

Here are some typical problems with bad rubrics.

- They don't have a label for the high and low ends of a scale.
- They have too many quality categories. How do you grade "spelling" on a 1-10 scale?
- They include too many factors in a single criterion. For example, if you put "uses the five W's and one H," what do you do if the student includes all but one? All but two?
- They don't have components or criteria of equal weight or they are missing some essentials.
- They don't use the same criteria or components in all categories.

There are many issues you should think about when developing a really fine "Cadillac" of a grading rubric. A "Cadillac" rubric has a tremendous level of detail in each quality category. They take a long time to develop, but are well worth the effort. In the long run they save you time because you aren't writing the same comments over and over on student papers!

On the following pages are examples of other "decent" grading rubrics. I say "decent" because rubrics always seem like they can be improved! You find this out when you are grading projects or papers, so keep some notes while grading so you can make improvements on your rubrics later.

Rubrics can be developed for grading portfolios in education, projects in machine tool engineering, papers in astronomy, a public speech, or almost anything which can be broken down into sensible quality categories, by necessary components or criteria.

The "Cadillac" rubric on the following page is for a beginning essay in English composition. Only the first row is completed, as a sample. As students progress, this rubric would change and include more elements. Rubrics used at the end of a semester should be far more complicated than those used at the beginning.

Rubrics can be adapted to any subject area. You should weight the components (assign points to individual cells.) Weighting helps make students aware that, while some elements are more important than others, they need all elements for a good, complete project (see examples, pp. 55-57.)

# Sample "Cadillac" Grading Rubric

**First**, identify the major components or criteria you'll be using—the essentials—with approximately equal importance.

**Second**, decide how many quality categories to use. This number may change as you're writing your descriptions and find some items don't fit your scheme. Then you'll have to revise. Remember: rubrics take some time! You may be used to five categories (A, B, C, D, F), but those shades of difference seem very difficult across all components. I recommend four divisions, but three are appropriate for some components. Also, you can have two sections on your form, with different scales, one with more categories and one with fewer. Just separate the sections and anchor the scales individually.

| Major Components | 1 — *Unacceptable: needs significant improvement or aspects are missing* | 2 — *Unacceptable: needs some improvement* | 3 — *Acceptable* | 4 — *Good: shows full control over this aspect* |
|---|---|---|---|---|
| **Introduction** | ☐ **Thesis** missing or not understandable<br>☐ Reader is probably **confused**<br>☐ No hook evident | ☐ **Thesis** might confuse or mislead reader<br>☐ Several sentences **confuse or off target**<br>☐ Lacks a sufficient **hook** to intrigue reader | ☐ **Thesis** there but not laser clear, or too simplistic<br>☐ Some sentences a bit **confusing or off target**<br>☐ Not quite as **hooking** (might lack examples/appeal) | ☐ Clear **thesis**; depth evident<br>☐ **No confusing sentences**—all are on target<br>☐ **Hooks** reader |
| **Body** | | | | |
| **Conclusion** | | | | |
| **Spelling, Grammar, Syntax** | | | | |
| **Coherence** | | | | |
| **Unity** | | | | |

**Third**, decide on the aspects to judge for each component. At the beginning, don't make it too complex.

As you teach additional aspects, add them to your rubrics. When developing a rubric, I find it useful to start with the A paper; in this case, what elements does the A paper contain in an introduction?

**Fourth**, carry the same identical aspects across all the quality categories. If you use the word "hook" under any category, then use it under all categories. Do not put elements into any one category that you don't put into all the others.

*Important:* When grading, check off what a student does well in each box. This is a way to provide lots of specific feedback without writing a note to each student.

## Essay: Descriptive Mode
(Sample here includes only a few components of the original rubric. Notes for student are in italics.)

| Component | 0 | 1 | 2 | 3 | Weight and Total Points |
|---|---|---|---|---|---|
| | | | | Well done; shows clear control in this area | |
| | Not Present | Attempt made, but still needs polish and consistency | Adequate; shows understanding but not full control yet | | |
| Clear thesis statement in opening paragraph | Which sentence is your thesis? I'm stumped as to direction essay will go. | | | | X2 *Points: 0* |
| Opening "hooks" reader | | | Example is pretty compelling—reader wants to know more. | | X1 *Points : 2* |
| Coherence within paragraphs (one topic per paragraph; varied sentence structure) | | Half of your paragraphs have topic sentences, half don't— fair sentence variety. | | | X3 *Points: 3* |
| Etc. | | | | | |

Rubric with points already weighted in cells

| Component | Not Present | Attempt made, but still needs polish and consistency | Adequate; shows understanding but not full control yet | Well done; shows clear control in this area | Total Points |
|---|---|---|---|---|---|
| Clear thesis statement in opening paragraph | 0 | 2 | 4 | 6 | /6 |
| Opening "hooks" reader | 0 | 1 | 2 | 3 | /3 |
| Coherence within paragraphs (one topic per paragraph; varied sentence structure) | 0 | 2 *Half of your paragraphs have topic sentences, half don't—fair sentence variety.* | 4 | 6 | 2/6 |

## Grading Rubrics Simplified

Below is an example of a simple grading rubric for a final paper. If you break down the components enough and develop sufficiently descriptive quality category headings, you can actually do without individual descriptions under each quality category. This type of rubric is a good one to start on if you aren't familiar with rubrics, although be aware that it is *not* as good as a full descriptive rubric. Still, *if* you have given students adequate instruction in each component, they should understand the difference between "adequate" and "good."

### Final Paper Criteria—English Composition

| | Missing, or nearly missing; or did not meet assignment parameters | Trying, but inadequate or many errors | Acceptable, but not very polished; still some errors or lack of control | Good, very few errors— shows real skill developing; good control exhibited |
|---|---|---|---|---|
| Title page—MLA style | ❏ | ❏ | ❏ | ❏ |
| Meets all assignment criteria | ❏ | ❏ | ❏ | ❏ |
| **Clear thesis** statement in opening | ❏ | ❏ | ❏ | ❏ |
| Opening engages reader | ❏ | ❏ | ❏ | ❏ |
| Clear topic sentences/each paragraph | ❏ | ❏ | ❏ | ❏ |
| Good **coherence** within paragraphs | ❏ | ❏ | ❏ | ❏ |
| Good transitions between paragraphs | ❏ | ❏ | ❏ | ❏ |
| Overall paper **unity** | ❏ | ❏ | ❏ | ❏ |
| **Mature development of argument** | ❏ | ❏ | ❏ | ❏ |
| Both pros/cons well developed | ❏ | ❏ | ❏ | ❏ |
| Persuasive conclusion | ❏ | ❏ | ❏ | ❏ |
| **Grammar/spelling/punctuation** | ❏ | ❏ | ❏ | ❏ |
| **Variety of sentence structures** | ❏ | ❏ | ❏ | ❏ |
| **MLA format** followed throughout for paraphrasing, citations, quotes | ❏ | ❏ | ❏ | ❏ |
| Four references (attached) | ❏ | ❏ | ❏ | ❏ |
| Reference page in MLA style | ❏ | ❏ | ❏ | ❏ |

All the above items were considered in grading your final research paper. Of particular weight are the **bold** items. Comments:

This type of rubric still allows you to approach the paper holistically; it just shows how you assessed it. Add comments to summarize your impressions. When you check the rubric boxes, students get a clear idea of what they need to improve and what they're doing well.

Note the lack of an excellent category. Few student papers are really excellent. If one is, you can add ++++ beside the good checkbox. We want to encourage all students to improve.

Again, a reminder: *always* hand rubrics out before assignment is due! They serve as guidelines and prompts for students.

## Enforcing Expectations: Headers for Rubrics
What do you do with a paper that doesn't meet the guidelines you set forth? That's an individual decision—and it causes a lot of grief, particularly when students come up and say, "You never told me ... XXX." This is a problem with any verbal instructions: not all of the students are paying attention.

To solve this problem, I've added a header to my rubrics (see p. 60). When I pass out this grading rubric with the syllabus and when I go over it as I explain the assignment, students know I'm serious about what I want them to do.

That's how you get their attention. Then, of course, you need to follow through and do what you say. So, use a smaller version for the very first paper, *follow* your own rules, and allow students to resubmit the paper for full points. This shows that you're serious about the parameters. Many students are not used to being held accountable for completing an assignment as assigned.

## Evaluating Group Work With Rubrics
Some students hate group projects. No, "hate" is too mild a word. Some students absolutely *loathe* group projects.

**Students:** The rubric will be used to grade your paper. *But* in order for me to even start grading it, it must meet all the following parameters:

1. Typed, double-spaced, stapled, and *turned in on time*
   - ❑ Yes (continue with grading)
   - ❑ No (stop grading here – score: 0%)

2. Right *number* (five) and *types* of references used (web, book, interview); clearly cited on a Works Cited page
   - ❑ Yes (continue with grading)
   - ❑ No (stop grading here – score: 0%)

3. All sources are attached *and* areas quoted or paraphrased *highlighted*
   - ❑ Yes (continue with grading)
   - ❑ No (stop grading here – score: 0%)

4. MLA format used throughout
   - ❑ Yes (continue with grading)
   - ❑ No (stop grading here – score: 0%)

5. Length: *over* five pages, *excluding* Title Page and Works Cited page
   - ❑ Yes (continue with grading)
   - ❑ No (stop grading here – score: 0%)

Why? Sometimes students are just shy, but usually it is because the grading never seems fair. The group members who want an A end up doing most of the work and group members who hardly participate at all get to go along for the ride and usually end up with a grade they don't deserve. This happens throughout the educational system, including graduate school. So how can you fairly evaluate group work?

First, set the project up for fairness. Here are some suggestions.

- Address the issues inherent in group work when you introduce the project. Discuss the "perfect" group and the truly "dysfunctional" group. Talk about what expectations group members have for one another and how they can head off or report problems. Make the consequences for being a sluggard obvious.

- Establish firm roles and written expectations for each role or make this the first assignment for the group. The members can develop a little contract. Each member should sign on the dotted line, literally, to participate at "x" level. Members need to know clearly what is expected of them.

- Set a minimum number of meetings acceptable. Have each group member submit a journal entry from each meeting summarizing his or her input and the meeting. They should turn these in throughout the project, usually weekly or biweekly, not just at the end.

- When you introduce the project, hand students the form you will use to evaluate their project and the forms they will use to evaluate the contribution of each member. Both forms can be rubrics.

- Consider dividing the project grade into individual and group contribution points, rather than grade the group only. For example, each student does a paper and each group does a presentation.

- If the project involves a presentation and you want every member to speak, not just the "brave and polished" one, make that clear ahead of time and put it on your grading rubric.

- Give some time during class for groups to coordinate. *Find out* which students commute or work. Don't just assign a group project and expect all of your students to have time to meet outside of class.

- Realize that some students are just learning to function within a group. Most will have difficulty handling group dynamics. Don't expect them to already know how to do this well. Give guidance and help along the way.

Second, use self-evaluation and group evaluation rubrics for all group members. Here are some suggestions.

- Have each group member evaluate the contributions of each of the others to the project. Design your rubrics so students can rate behaviors as objectively as possible.

- Below is a simple Likert scale. It is not very objective, but I've seen it in use. Just don't use it as the sole way you ask group members to grade each other! If you use items like this, put them at the end of your rubric.

**Bad example:**

_____*Name*_____ Did Not Contribute  1  2  3  4  5  Contributed A Lot

- Before such general items as the one above, it's best to ask several questions about specific issues, such as number of meetings attended, number of articles found, percentage of final presentation written, or contributions under a number of headings:

Number of meetings we held during project development: _____

My name: _____
Circle number of meetings I attended for the full length.
1  2  3  4  5  6  7  8

Member's name: _____
Circle number of meetings he/she attended for the full length.
1  2  3  4  5  6  7  8

Member's name: _____
Circle number of research articles he/she contributed to the project.
1  2  3  4  5  6  7  8

- Have students complete the group evaluation forms in class so they don't "consult" each other. That way, you'll be able to compare the grades given to each student by the members of his or her group.

- If you ask group members to grade each other, give them a clear rubric with multiple behavioral components, rather than asking them to assign grades holistically.

- Finally, at the close of the project, have group members write individual journal entries or a reflective paper, evaluating what they learned, what went well, and what barriers arose. Guide their reflection with a set of questions to answer. These reflections will be invaluable as you improve your abilities to design and evaluate group projects.

# Indirect Measures of Student Learning

## Formative Indirect Measures of Learning Environments
Why use formative indirect assessment?

This type of assessment does not assess student learning outcomes directly. It looks at the learning environment under your control. If done about a third of the way into the term, these measures can give you a glimpse into how students view your class overall, in time to change some things. The assumption is that change might then improve student learning outcomes. If you really don't want to know student perceptions of your class in general or you won't change anything, it's best not to do formative indirect assessment!

To assess the learning environment holistically, ask the students to answer two questions: (1) What are the five best things about this class? (2) What are the five things about this class that you'd most like to see improved to help you learn more?

- You can put students into small groups or have them answer individually. Allow 20 minutes from beginning to end of exercise.

- Ask them to be serious. Tell them you can't change the time of day or the fact that the cafeteria doesn't have Starbucks. Tell them this is their chance to help you set up the best possible learning environment and you want serious input.

- If you're going to devote class time to this, leave the room while they're answering the questions and leave a student in charge. Just be sure to explain the task well first and tell them you'll be coming back. If you don't want to devote class time, have students take the questions home, type up their answers, and bring them to the next session. Some students are extremely edgy about being identified by their handwriting. Either way, have a big envelope for them to put their answers in.

- Examine the responses in private (not in class) to identify trends or particularly good suggestions and prepare to address any major issues.

Students will be waiting for something to change. If there is a big issue, they'll want you to address it directly. If they see no change, this will damage your credibility. If you change anything (your handwriting, timing of breaks, worksheets for videos, clarity of due dates, number of test items—the list goes on and on), it works for you.

- Be open to the fact that student perceptions will not always match yours. You cannot please everyone; there will be unhappy students in every class. But don't dismiss negative comments out-of-hand. There may be a grain of truth in all of them. Although, some suggestions are just plain wrong, groups of like comments usually have some truth in them.

- Important: Don't be defensive with your students! Respectfully acknowledge concerns and patterns and tell how you will address them. Responding respectfully is the key to having formative indirect measures work to help you improve.

## Student-Designed Rubrics

Rubrics aren't just for teachers anymore. Students can design rubrics as projects, especially culminating projects. To design a rubric they must have a solid base of knowledge and then operate at Bloom's synthesis and evaluation levels. Student-designed rubrics can become another way to evaluate learning outcomes.

Students can design rubrics successfully in many different subject areas. In child development, students should be able to design rubrics for evaluating the safety of toys for toddlers, or for evaualting a lesson plan for three-year-olds. If they cannot figure out all the elements that need to be considered for either of these projects, then something has been missed in their education. By the end of the semester a nutrition student should be able to develop a rubric to evaluate a food plan for a diabetic. A management student should be able to develop a rubric to evaluate a strategic planning session. A special education student should be able to develop a rubric to evaluate an Individual Education Plan (IEP) for a disabled student.

You can use student-designed rubrics in either a formative or summative manner. The difference is whether or not you use the information you gather from them solely as feedback, or if you grade the rubrics. In either case, you need to train students to develop them first.

Show students several rubrics and discuss the elements that make a good one. Then I want to recommend a terrific project to cement their understanding: developing a "potato" rubric. Yes. Potatoes. Bring in a bunch of different size potatoes in every possible shape, some battered, some growing eyes, some green, some gorgeous. Give your students the assignment of designing a rubric any 14-year-old could use to purchase an excellent baking potato. Small groups will fly into this assignment and have fun while actually learning about the complexity of developing a rubric. Give out large sheets of paper to draw on and conduct a whole group examination/evaluation of each finished rubric. By the time students have processed all the different rubrics and noted the strengths and weaknesses of each, they will be ready to tackle a much more complex project in their subject area. The "Potato Rubric" exemplifies a challenging, focused, active learning activity.

### Indirect Measures for Specific Projects
I find that "mini" measures on specific projects or teaching techniques give me a wealth of important information. Also, it's easy to create and use them.

The "Happy Faces" rubric (p. 66) works really well for a brief measure of projects, videos, etc. Use two or three questions only. This assessment takes about a minute tops and provides valuable input.

## Summative Indirect Measures

### Homegrown and Institutional Tools
At the course level, summative indirect assessment measures usually boil down to one thing: faculty evaluation forms that include items regarding student outcomes. These forms are discussed at length in the next section.

At the institutional level, many forms of indirect summative assessment are probably taking place, but generally they are not your concern. Certainly, if you are asked to help make an institutional survey available to your students during a class period, you want to cooperate, but beyond that modest contribution, you probably won't be involved.

**Please assess the video we just saw:**

The video clarified some issues for me.

The video worksheet was helpful
to focus my attention.

Use this video again next semester.

How could this activity be improved?

(Yes, some students won't answer this question because you could identify
them by their handwriting, but they will be in the minority since the question
targets one specific activity: it doesn't ask for negative comments about the
course in general.)

**Please give me some input on the jigsaw method we used in class.**

The jigsaw seemed to get more
people directly involved.

The jigsaw worked well to
help me learn the material.

I'd like to use this again this semester.

How could this activity be improved?

You can perform your own summative indirect measures by designing simple questionnaires to ask students how much they have learned, in what areas they have learned the most, etc. These are truly indirect, because they measure perceptions, not performance.

Perceptions are important, of course. If students don't see their progress the same way you see it (through grading their work), then perhaps you need to provide some system to enable them to see it more accurately. Or perhaps you need to consider whether there's a discrepancy between what you see as important for them to learn and what they see as important.

Below is a good way to design this type of measure. Remember: they only elicit perceptions; they do not provide a true measure of learning. But they help verify patterns you find in student papers and on final tests.

Use with caution. Perceptions are frequently not reality.

| Rate your knowledge level on the first day of class. | | | | | | Rate your knowledge level on the last day of class. | | | | |
|---|---|---|---|---|---|---|---|---|---|---|
| Very Low | | | | Fairly High | | Very Low | | | | Fairly High |
| 1 | 2 | 3 | 4 | 5 | Ability to develop a clear thesis statement | 1 | 2 | 3 | 4 | 5 |
| 1 | 2 | 3 | 4 | 5 | Ability to proofread my own work and catch errors | 1 | 2 | 3 | 4 | 5 |

## Indirect Measures of You! (Faculty Evaluations)

Instructors who are novices often have questions about institutional faculty evaluations. Here are some of the most common questions—and answers.

- *Where do I get them?* Usually they miraculously appear in your mailbox, with instructions. If they don't appear, ask the department secretary or your faculty contact how to get them.

- *Should I use them?* Of course! First, you might not have an option if you want to teach at the college again. Second, they may give you some valuable information—maybe, depending upon how they are designed.

- *Are they a personality contest?* Not usually. You will have enough solid, serious students in your classes to keep the focus on teaching proficiency and away from teacher personality.

- *When do I give them?* Not on the day of the final test. Not on a day when the class has been particularly boring. Not one minute before the bell rings. Usually the instructions say, "Before the end of the semester," so choose your day wisely. After all, you want the best possible results to support your case for more future classes or tenure.

- *How much time do I allow?* This depends upon the length of the form. But schedule 20 minutes, usually at the end of class.

Before using the forms, ask to look over the questions. All evaluation forms are not created equal. Some are truly awful, actually, or so general that the feedback is of little value. But many colleges let instructors add questions. If that's true where you're teaching, design some questions that serve your needs. There may be timelines involved here, so inquire early about this.

Protect student privacy at all times. If the college does not provide a sealable envelope for the completed forms, bring your own. Always put a student in charge and leave the room. Don't hover around while your students are trying to evaluate you! Assign a student to take the forms to the drop-off point. *Never* handle the completed forms yourself.

### The Visit from Your Supervisor

Expect your supervisor to observe your teaching at least once a term when you are new at a college. These observations are usually scheduled in advance.

Some supervisors "forget" to observe their instructors. As mentioned earlier, many are extremely busy (or lazy ... or disorganized ... or negligent). If your supervisor "forgets," this is not necessarily a good thing. If you are a good instructor, you want to be observed! If your supervisor does not observe your teaching, any future references will be based only on student evaluations and opinions. *Invite* your supervisor to come observe you.

*Plan ahead* for the observation. Ask if you can see what form (if any) your supervisor will be using to observe you. Make certain that everything will run smoothly—and don't spend half the period testing. Show your stuff!

# Checklist: Assessment

**General:**

❏ Locate your department's assessment plan and check to make sure you're following it, if required.

❏ Ask your mentor or another faculty member for samples of his or her grading rubrics. (Ask if they mind sharing, of course!)

**Formative:**

❏ Decide which major concepts you should use formative direct assessment on. Schedule time into the syllabus for these classroom assessment techniques. Have copies ready to use.

❏ Design several indirect formative assessments for specific activities and projects you want to evaluate for effectiveness. Have copies ready to use.

❏ Design "in-progress" evaluation forms for group projects. (These allow group members to get feedback from each other as they progress through a project.)

❏ Check the library or teaching resource center for books on classroom assessment techniques.

**Summative:**

❏ Plan for summative assessments over specific objectives multiple times during the term, maybe over each chapter or two.

❏ Design comprehensive summative tests and projects for the end of the course that include several major objectives.

❏ Design the evaluation means for all summative assessments. Be prepared to hand copies out to students ahead of time.

❏ Locate faculty evaluation forms and review them. Find out if you can add questions.

❏ If you cannot alter the standard faculty evaluation form, design your own questions for your students and put together the appropriate package to have them returned to you after you've posted grades.

❏ Prepare for your supervisor to observe you. Request it.

# Motivating Students

Why aren't my students coming to class?

This is a frequent question for new instructors. You have to learn to deal with poor attendance in your own way. At one extreme is an economics professor who told me, "I couldn't care less if students come to class. If they pass the tests, that tells me they know the material and that's what I want." At the other extreme was a professor of small group communication: "It's a little hard to hold a small group discussion if a different part of the group is consistently missing. I want them there every single day. My whole class design requires daily participation."

Most instructors were successful as students. They generally liked school, liked to learn, and probably attended class regularly because they were engaged—or at least worried about their grades.

Many of our students are not like that. It's a new age. Understanding and applying some basic principles of motivation in your classes is essential to setting up situations that enhance student learning. You might think students should come to class because they'll learn something. However, they might need a lot more incentive.

## Expectancy–Value Theory

Why *will* students come to class? Basic Expectancy–Value theory can help us answer that question.

There has to be something in it for them (value) and they have to feel they have a chance to succeed (expectancy). If either component is missing, students will lack motivation.

This important theory can help us understand student motivation and give us clues about how to enhance it. According to the basic expectancy–value theory (Allan Wigfield and Jacquelynne S. Eccles, editors, *Development of Achievement Motivation,* Academic Press, San Diego, 2001), students consider three questions:

- "Is reaching the goal of any value to me?"
- "Can I reach the goal if I put forth the effort? Can I expect success in this class?"
- "What's the cost to me—in effort, in time, in energy, in risk to self-esteem? What else could I be doing with my time that I'll have to give up?"

So, to feel motivated:

- Students have to perceive a real value to them for reaching the goal.
- Students have to feel they can succeed.
- Success must be worth the costs to them in energy and time.

This means that you need to do the following:

- Build value into each class through a variety of means.
- Engage your students through active learning techniques.
- Use assessment and feedback astutely to help them succeed.
- Build a welcoming and accepting class atmosphere.

## Conceptions of Ability Theory

My Ph.D. dissertation dealt with college students' conceptions of ability. I still find this a fascinating area, especially because it is one that impacts student effort and instructors have such influence over it.

Here are the basics, in simple terms. For the details, you can read the numerous publications of Carol S. Dweck, Ellen L. Leggett, and Jacquelynne Eccles from 1983 to the present.

Students have a conception about the nature of ability. That conception impacts how much effort they put forth when they hit a "bump" in the road, like failing a test.

These are the two basic conceptions of ability:

- Entity—Students believe, "I have a cup's worth of ability. It is a set size. Whether the cup is large (gifted) or small, it can't enlarge. Ability is not malleable. So I have just 'so much' math ability. When I hit failure, I must have reached the limit of my cup. To put forth more effort is useless and will only hurt my self-esteem. If I don't study, at least I can say, 'I failed because I didn't study,' which saves face."

- Incremental—Students believe, "Ability is like an unpoppable balloon: the more effort I put forth, the bigger the balloon gets and the more ability I develop. So, when I hit failure, that's a clue I need to put forth more effort. I expect that effort will build my ability and failure is not a clue that I'm 'at my limit.' Ability is malleable."

Robert Wood and Albert Bandura did a fascinating study with graduate students and conceptions of ability ("Social Cognitive Theory of Organizational Management," *Academy of Management Review*, 14:3, 1989, pp. 361-384). On a complex organizational management task, students who had been "set up" to believe the Entity view rapidly faltered under failure conditions. Students who had been "set up" to believe the Incremental view did not falter, made better decisions, and showed more positive emotions. This is what we want!

Conceptions of ability can vary over subject areas. English and math, in particular, are areas where some students feel that success happens through some "special talent."

*Instructors can set up an* entity *atmosphere or an* incremental *atmosphere!* It's up to you.

On the first day, explain the two conceptions of ability to your students. Talk with them about their conceptions about what it takes to do well in your subject. Give them ample examples of people who did not do well in high school but who thrived in college when they started to understand that *effort*, not talent alone, makes for success. Help them understand that people learn at different speeds, but with effort almost everyone can attain the knowledge he or she needs in any subject area.

Students are fascinated with this theory. Explaining it helps them question their own beliefs and sometimes change poor behaviors.

## Questions to Ask Yourself

### No Student Left Behind?
Impossible task. If your success as an instructor is heavily linked to every student succeeding in your courses, then you are doomed to wringing your hands in anguish. You cannot care more about your students' education than they care about it themselves.

Your goal should be to set up the best possible learning environment, give feedback, do formative assessment and make adjustments, teach clearly, grade fairly, and motivate as well as you can. The rest is up to your students: it's their responsibility. You can't run the race for them.

However, if you're failing a lot of your students every semester ... or giving "A" grades to way too many of them, you need to examine your expectations, your teaching, and your assessment.

Are students productively involved in cognitively demanding ways?

That's probably the most important question of all. If you use active learning techniques that engage your students at the higher levels of Bloom's taxonomy, you will be involving them as active participants. Make sure you use the higher levels of Bloom, however, because students hate work that just keeps them busy but doesn't help them learn. Challenge their minds!

## Are My Students Bored?
To answer that question, ask two more.

*Am I boring?*

Possibly! Videotape yourself and see if you would sleep through your own class. Learn to modulate your voice, use gestures, walk around, be engaging. Fabulous teachers usually do have a bit of theater in them or so it seems because they're so enthusiastic about their subject.

*Is my course boring?*

Possibly! Use formative assessment and find out. If students feel class is boring, find out what to fix. If you use active learning techniques, this is not going to be a problem.

## Do I Know the Material?
Few things are more de-motivating to students than an instructor they don't consider credible. Know the material—and know it well.

Don't get into situations where you don't really know the material well enough. Being an expert is *not* the same thing as having answers to everything. Usually it is people who are unsure of their knowledge who can't say, "I don't know." Experts actually know they can't answer everything that comes up.

Keep learning. Continue to develop professionally. Students can generally pick out a phony and they feel insulted.

## Is My Course Challenging Enough?

Easy classes are actually de-motivating, especially to fast learners. No one respects them, though word gets around and students may still take them for the easy grade.

## Is My Course Too Challenging?

Remember: students have to think they have a good chance at success. Courses that are way over their heads aren't likely to inspire good attendance or effort. For some subjects, the best way to gauge the appropriate level of challenge is to test students during the first week on the material you feel is prerequisite to taking your course and the material you might cover in the first month. This will help you set the right challenge level as well as provide extra help to students who don't quite grasp something essential. It will also help you guide some students out of your course and into a lower-level course where they can succeed.

## Am I Building Value Connections?

It is your responsibility to show your students the value of your subject. It's not enough that it fascinates you! On the first day, ask students to write down their majors, interests, and questions they have about the subject, as well as goals for the class. Go over these privately and try hard to build connections to major areas of interest within your lesson designs. Just a one-minute linkage per day will do wonders for motivation. As you build your connections, students will see ways to build their own. This is a wonderful gift you'll be modeling for them.

## Why Don't They Get This? Am I Confusing?

Maybe! Formative assessment will help you find out. Use it. If you do a "What's Confusing?" CAT and three-fourths of your students are lost, look to how you structure your lessons. You may need to change things.

Are you skipping what you think is too elementary? Maybe it is for you, but not for them. Use more examples. Break the concept into smaller parts. Build links more deliberately between old and new information. Try a new approach.

Remember: don't expect different results if you keep doing the same old things! Most important, don't blame the students if most of them are confused.

## Is Class Fun?

No, class doesn't have to be "fun," but humor helps at times. Just be careful that your humor is appropriate. You are in a power position even if you try not to be: teasing humor might be taken poorly by some students.

Games are a good, solid source of fun. You can access a free "Jeopardy" template online and it works beautifully for review sessions in most subjects. I've used it many times and assigned bonus points for the winning team—one situation in which competition among groups seems to be OK. I usually give points for first, second, and third places, so almost every group wins.

## Have I Built Choice into My Classes?

This won't work for all classes, but it does work for most. Allow as much choice as possible, because students are more motivated to work on problems or issues they choose for themselves. Where can you build choice into your classes?

## Do I Reward Effort?

This is a big issue in some classes, especially math. What if a student does a complicated problem correctly right up until the last decimal point? Is it all wrong? Or do you give partial credit? Obviously that depends. One solution is to give partial credit for the first half of a semester with the clear understanding that credit for process will stop at midterm.

You have to answer this question yourself. It is definitely worth pondering and answering because how you treat effort can affect motivation, especially as we take uncertain learners into higher levels of performance.

## What Is the Class Atmosphere?

Do students feel free to ask questions? Of course you might say they *should* feel free, but do they really? Again, this is a formative assessment issue, an indirect measures question.

If you ever put a student down rudely for a "stupid" question or an incorrect answer or allow other students to do this, you will kill the positive class atmosphere so necessary to a true learning environment. Disruptive students who monopolize or are rude to you or others also kill the class atmosphere. You must deal with such students directly and rapidly. You need to stay in charge of creating a good environment.

When bringing something into class, such as a film, remember you have no job security. It's best to choose wisely and not use anything that could easily be considered offensive or controversial (*extreme* violence, racism, sexism, and so forth). If a student complains about an adjunct or a new instructor "setting up a hostile learning environment," that situation has potentially different consequences than for a faculty member with tenure.

## Is Anxiety Too High?

A high level of anxiety hurts performance and motivation. Under high-anxiety conditions, people can't think as clearly. High anxiety can come when a test has high stakes (the course grade rides on only one or two tests), when difficult questions put students on the spot in front of their peers, or when expectations and procedures are not clear enough.

You can keep anxiety from rising too high by providing study guides, making your expectations clear, allowing plenty of time to perform, and using better questioning techniques.

Be careful with competition. I've found that instructors who like competition themselves almost always tend to think that competition helps motivate students. In general, not so. Competition generally diminishes motivation.

## Do I Communicate My Joy in Teaching?

Teaching is a fabulous job. It's a privilege to be able to engage minds in learning. Communicate this! Convey your feelings for what you do.

And if you don't really feel this way, maybe this isn't the profession for you. Students sense when instructors would really rather be doing something other than teaching. Students are spending their money to be in your class. They want you to want to be there, too.

## Incentives, Rewards, and a Little Punishment

After you have set up the best possible class environment, a slightly behavioral approach to motivation may add that little extra push for attendance. Most instructors use some system of incentives, rewards, and punishments, even if they don't call them by those names.

First, ask yourself if it's OK with you if students can pass your class without attending. If they can, this means you must be teaching straight out of a textbook, adding nothing new, and using only the test bank items. This is rather like a correspondence course. Bright students might skip frequently if there's no reason for them to come except on test days. They can read and memorize the book by themselves.

Don't make attendance mandatory for your own ego; it should be mandatory because students need to be there to get something out of the class and to contribute to a learning community of peers. If you aren't going to provide these opportunities for students, then why force them to show up when you're not giving a test?

*But,* if you're going to set up a participatory, active environment and you want your students to show up regularly, try the following behavioral techniques.

- Continuous reinforcement helps establish a behavior. Give points just for showing up and participating in the in-class activities for the first six or so sessions.

- Intermittent reinforcement helps sustain a behavior. This is why people like to continuously pull on those one-armed gambling bandits. They know there will be reinforcement, but they don't know when. After a period of reinforcing attendance continuously, start reinforcing intermittently.

- Here's a *great* idea. A philosophy professor I knew had an extremely successful idea for providing intermittent reinforcement for attendance. He had a big, bold spinner wheel with various points from one to 10 on it. Each day he made a production out of having a student spin the wheel—it took 30 seconds tops—to set the points available for the in-class activity for the day. Students cheered and hooted and stomped while the wheel spun, getting their physiology all geared up for a rousing lecture on Plato.

- Grade those in-class activities. Don't just automatically give every student points for doing the work any which way. If you don't consider quality, the quality will rapidly decline for the whole class. If the wheel spins and eight points are available, dole them out somewhat generously, but still according to merit. Some students will not get full points and they are likely to put out more effort next time.

- Make in-class activities a significant portion of the course grade. Do not allow make-ups on in-class activities unless students have a written medical or military excuse. The only way to get the points, then, is to come to class. Hold firm to this rule. Put this information in the syllabus!

- Test frequently. I give a quiz a week, over one chapter. I do not allow make-ups unless students have a medical or military excuse. Put all this information in the syllabus!

- Drop the lowest two or three in-class activities or test scores. This avoids a lot of hassles with excuses from funerals, etc. This way students can blow a couple of tests or miss two or three classes— "no-harm, no foul."

- Supplement the textbook information. Give information in class that is an addition to the textbook and then be sure to include it on the tests. Regularly or randomly, this helps. Besides, you are supposed to be an expert: you should be able to add to the text. The key is to test over the new material you add.

- Drop grades if students don't attend. For some classes, like counseling or interpersonal skills, tests or written in-class products may not be

frequent enough to use as an incentive. If class participation is
critical to the whole design of your course, try setting a straight
attendance policy which reflects that importance. "Miss four classes
and your grade drops one letter grade. Miss five classes, two letter
grades." I would not use this tactic, however, in classes where you
can test frequently.

## How to Annoy Students

Teachers annoy students when they do these things:

- They read the syllabus on day one word for word, all class—boring!
- They tell students on day one how many will fail the course.
- They say something is boring, as in "This chapter is really boring,
  but ...."
- They spend too much time taking roll each day.
- They take too long to pass out papers.
- They take too much time getting the activities organized.
- They spend too much time dealing with recalcitrant technology.
- They talk about their personal lives when this is a tangent.
- They do not handle rude or disruptive students.
- They let some students dominate discussions.
- They tolerate slackers and sleepers.
- They're disorganized and take class time to put their notes in order.
- They're unable to explain difficult concepts clearly and carefully.
- They're defensive and they don't really answer questions.
- They never ask students what they think.
- They come to class late—regularly.
- They leave class early—regularly.
- They offer nothing new, teaching straight from the text.
- They make students feel stupid.
- They use a tone of voice that's anything but professional.
- They berate the class and anger good students.
- They act like they'd rather be doing anything else but teaching.

- They talk about how poorly they get paid.
- They complain about the administration.
- They lecture with PowerPoint for three hours in a dark room.
- They give pure lectures that drone on and on.
- They don't take breaks in long classes.
- They speak in monotones and/or not loud enough.
- They don't write clearly.
- They use active learning activities that seem silly, beneath their dignity.
- They use inappropriate humor and think they're being funny.

## Effective Teachers

Here are some behaviors that make teachers effective:

- They know their subject matter thoroughly.
- They plan their course goals, objectives, and activities.
- They're clear and organized.
- They involve students actively in learning.
- They display warmth and enthusiasm.
- They engage students in critical thinking.
- They plan their questioning in advance.
- They let their students know they love teaching.
- They let their students know they love their subject area.
- They continually strive to gather information from their students.
- They use student feedback to improve their teaching skills.
- They teach holistically, embedding skills, knowledge, attitudes, and behaviors to be learned within real applications, remembering the whole person.

# Getting Things Right at the Start

## Professionalism

Teachers are generally social animals. We prefer that people enjoy us, but this is not the target outcome for your class; the outcome is student learning. Your role is not to be a "buddy," so don't act that way. It is hard to grade "friends" fairly. And, if you assume the role of "buddy," students will have very different expectations of you.

Maintain a professional, respectful, friendly presence. That doesn't mean you can't also be silly at times and throw out candy to groups with the best answers to questions, but it does mean establishing and maintaining professional boundaries. You can still share personal stories that are appropriate to the subject at hand or tell students you're having a "bad day." Students want you to be a fully human being, but students also have expectations for college instructors. When you fit their image of a professional college instructor, they know what to expect and are actually more comfortable.

## Learn Your Students' Names

Using your students' names in class and in the hall builds rapport. Learn them as rapidly as possible. One of the best ways to learn names is to hand out roll as a "blueprint" of your room and have students sign where they are sitting. You can refer to this sheet while conducting discussions or asking questions. (Make it large enough to be useful.) Always say "Hi" to students when you see them outside class.

## Use Ice-Breakers

Use some sort of ice-breaker on the first day of class, and perhaps on the second day also, because you'll have new students who have just added your course. There are books listing hundreds of ice-breaker activities, because corporate trainers use them a lot. The Web is also a great source.

Important: don't do anything that causes anxiety or creates a risk to self-esteem. No "trust me" activities with blindfolds. Nothing "touchy-feely." Nothing where students have to touch one another's bodies in any way. (I've seen some really awful ice-breakers!) Good ice-breakers get people to talk and share and laugh a bit. Silly ice-breakers with rubber chickens are a good way to loosen students up and get them to bond. Bonded classes of students who know each other's names function better and have better discussions!

## Prepare Your Students

Your students should know what to expect. Ease their concerns by discussing the syllabus and answering any questions about the course. The more organized you seem, the more comfortable students will be. Students want to leave a first class knowing what they will be expected to do, how they will be graded, how the class will be run, and what knowledge they should walk out with ... or need coming in. Fewer ambiguities means greater comfort. Make sure every student understands all the sections of your syllabus, particularly attendance policies, etc. Explain *why* these things are important. Build value for your subject and your class.

Part of preparing your students is finding out what they know. Test them at the start. This is very appropriate in some courses, where prior knowledge is essential. What you do with the results will vary: you may recommend a different section, you may start at a different point, you may hold a "catch-up" class for students who need to get up to the level, or you may provide background handouts.

## "Troublemakers" and Troubled Students

### Don't Tolerate Sleeping

Yes, sometimes students sleep in class. Don't tolerate it. This destroys class dynamics.

This potential problem is easy to handle if you address it on the first day, humorously. In my opening spiel I always mention that I don't tolerate sleepers. I tell my students, "I'll come kick you if you fall asleep in my class." This always gets a laugh—and then I tell them I'm quite serious ... but I'll only kick their foot, and not very hard ... the first time. Then I follow through.

Even though I have active classes, sometimes a student falls asleep during the brief lecture part. I walk over quietly, kick the sleeper's foot gently while the other students look on wide-eyed, and wake the sleeper up. If it happens a second time (rarely), I ask the sleeper to leave and go to bed. This works to keep all students awake.

### Don't Tolerate Rude Talking

On day one, discuss the issue of students chatting while you are talking or while other students are sharing. Let students discuss how annoying this is to them and solutions used in other classes—the good and the ugly. Come to a consensus on how to handle this problem—and then stick to it. Also assure students that they'll have plenty of time to discuss during group activities, so they can hold their casual thoughts for just a little while; they'll get time to share them. This helps!

## Defuse Troublemakers Early

Even in college, you'll have them occasionally—troublemakers. Some of them are mentally unstable, some are just immature, and others seem out to make your life miserable. You must deal with them swiftly and fairly or they will harm the learning environment for everyone. If you identify a potential troublemaker early, especially someone who looks like a "ringleader," sometimes you can go out of your way to give the student extra attention after or before class in an attempt to build personal rapport with him or her. Win that potential troublemaker over. Many times this will avert a problem.

Going head to head in class is not a good solution, since many troublemakers do not have the same social restraints as you, allowing them to come out ahead. Negative encounters between students and instructors are terribly disturbing to the other students. If you have trouble with a student, wait until class has ended. Then, take the student aside and discuss your feelings privately.

Use classic "I messages"—"I feel very disrespected when ...." Emphasize how his or her behavior is disrupting the class and how students have complained. Identify the specific behaviors that are disruptive. Don't just say, "You're being immature." Don't label the student. Prepare ahead of time so you can end by referring to policies in the student handbook regarding behavior and consequences. Be courteous and respectful even if the student is not. Specify what he or she needs to do to remain in the class. Ask what you need to do to help him or her adjust to class better. This will usually (not always) cure the situation. Keep notes of what transpired.

If you are uncomfortable approaching a student alone, ask your dean of instruction, dean of student affairs, or a counselor to accompany you. If a student seems dangerous in any way, hold this meeting in an administrator's office.

# Methods for Eliciting Questions

## Encouraging Students to Ask Questions

If you solicit questions only with "Does anyone have any questions?" at the end of a long lecture, don't expect good results! Only the boldest will ask anything! Break into questioning mode frequently so you don't lose any students.

Ask specific questions: "If the unconditioned stimulus were invisible, how could this experiment still work?" or "If the writer used second person, how would that change the tone of this short story—or would it?"

In order for students to ask questions, they have to feel free to show that they do not know. This is harder for some students than others—those who feel less sure of their abilities, who are very shy, or who care more about what others think of them. A good solution is to have "huddle time," where students form little groups for 30 seconds and come up with one or two questions. Then, no one is on the spot: the questions are coming from the group.

How you handle wrong answers or "dumb" questions becomes a signal (positive or negative) to other students. Never put a question down ... yet make sure students are not asking off-base questions for an inappropriate reason, such as to cause trouble or to delay. This is a delicate balancing act.

Encourage students to clarify their questions: "What specifically is the confusing part?" or "What part do you understand right now?" Encourage them to speculate a bit about the answer: "If you were going to speculate, what would you say? What do you think might be the first step, just guessing?"

Probe more deeply with better follow-up questions and encourage students to talk more when they question. This helps them learn.

The types of questions you answer also become a signal to the class.

In one graduate class, the professor answered a fact-based question like this: "That was in the textbook reading for today. Do you have any other questions, something beyond the readings that I can clarify?" The first time he responded that way the whole class froze. This was something new. He simply was not going to answer a knowledge-level question on info we could find ourselves if we'd read the chapters carefully. Believe me, he raised the bar considerably and forced students into deeper thinking ... at least about how we phrased our questions!

But, that was a graduate class. Undergraduates may need a little gentler approach: "What specifically confused you about the concept of XYZ in the book?" If the student says "the whole thing," then turn to the class and ask your other students to clarify the concept.

Some few students will actually attempt to be annoying or get attention (rare, but it happens) by asking questions over simple materials just to be talking. You want to curtail this activity; having their classmates develop the answer is a good solution.

## Formats for Interaction

### Seating Arrangement

Whether or not students are seated facing one another makes a staggering difference in classroom dynamics, attention, and discussion.

Don't settle for a room arrangement that lets some students "hide" or turn their backs to you. When there are tables with chairs set around them, it forces some students to sit with their backs to you or to sit at right angles to their note-taking materials. This arrangement isn't good. Rearrange.

Maximum interaction doesn't happen when students are looking at the backs of heads. If there is any way to alter the seating in your classroom to facilitate active discussion, do so.

Making either a large circle or a large U works well. Making two circles, one inside the other, works best for larger seminars or discussion-based classes. Making two U's, one inside the other, works best when the students still need to be looking up at you or the board for part of the class.

Try any arrangement that gets the students looking mostly eye to eye.

Arrange seating to facilitate the small group in-class activities you'll likely be using. You want a speedy transition from lecture to active learning activity. With the double-U setup, the students in the inner U can turn around rapidly and form groups with students in the outer U. There's no need to get up and mill about the room, wasting time. Then, to form new groups in the double-U arrangement, the inner students can just stand up and move over six seats left or right. Presto! Mostly new faces.

You might be very surprised how much the classroom dynamics change with a change in seating.

## Discussion
Discussion has probably been a prime teaching technique since the cave: "Gork, what do you feel was the best part of the buffalo hunt?" Discussion was certainly big with the Greeks, and, thousands of years later, most instructors are still using discussion.

Learning to wield this teaching tool effectively is certainly worth your planning and effort. And it definitely requires both planning and effort at the beginning. Good discussion rarely just happens.

What are the benefits of discussion?

- Students are directly involved.
- Students practice expressing themselves.
- Students get exposed to various viewpoints.
- Students can challenge each other's thinking and stretch themselves considerably.
- Students can problem-solve as a group and come to deeper understanding.

What are the downsides of discussion?

- Some students can dominate while others daydream. Solution: find ways to include everyone.
- Discussions can be unpredictable and very shallow. Solution: find questions that demand focus and depth. Keep probing.
- Discussions can be "the blind leading the blind"—ignorance shared and amplified. Solution: build knowledge first. Demand sources.

## Developing Good Discussions

*Plan ahead.* Work on your start-up questions, build student knowledge bases, and have an objective, an outcome—and communicate that outcome to students. A discussion isn't a free-for-all for opinions.

Train students in critical thinking first. Teach them to probe for clarity, depth, insight—to use critical thinking questions to expand discussions. For discussion questions, use only the upper levels of Bloom. Fact items don't work.

Encourage your students to pay attention to each other. Try a round-robin discussion. For whole classes, one student starts, the student sitting next to him or her reiterates the point and then adds to it. This continues around the class. Students start to pay attention to what others are saying! You can also do this in small groups (less threatening), with each group reporting back to the other students.

Ask two provocative questions students should be prepared to answer through their readings. Give them 10 minutes to answer them in writing, in class. Collect their answers. Then ask them how they responded. For the ensuing discussion to be good, the questions you ask must be open to multiple perspectives and have more than one answer.

Try challenge questions for groups. Prepare three questions, put students into groups, set a timer (a kitchen timer is a handy device), and let them discuss. Then, at the buzzer, stop the discussions and have a representative from each group report back to the other students. In small groups, students talk more with each other.

# Checklist: Motivation and Classroom Dynamics

**Preparations before class starts:**

❏ Plan a means to ask students their interests and goals so you can bring up examples during the semester that touch upon them (building value).

❏ Structure your classes to maximize participation.

❏ Develop a seating arrangement that facilitates discussion and attention.

❏ Find appropriate ice-breakers for days one and two.

❏ Learn the technology you'll be using so you don't waste time fiddling with it.

❏ Be highly organized so you don't waste any class time.

❏ Develop a method to learn names rapidly.

❏ Develop "new" material (not from the textbook) to add to each class period.

❏ Develop a couple of test items for each quiz over the material you're adding.

❏ Develop a presentation on entity and incremental conceptions of ability.

❏ Schedule your quizzes and tests in small, frequent bites.

❏ Be clear about attendance policies in the syllabus.

❏ Make in-class activities a significant portion of the grade.

❏ Develop a simple rubric for grading in-class activities.

❏ Develop a suitable intermittent reinforcement scheme and put it into the syllabus.

❏ Decide if you want to encourage attendance through punishment (like dropping grades). If so, put this into the syllabus clearly.

❏ Consider arranging for videotaping a couple of your classes.

❏ Write out good probing questions for specific lessons ahead of time.

❏ Plan your feedback system so students know how they are doing at all times.

❏ Plan several types of discussion and decide which lessons to use discussion with.

❏ Develop a lesson on critical thinking skills to give early in the semester.

**After the course gets rolling:**

❏ Learn your students' names rapidly and use them regularly.

❏ Use formative assessment of your teaching early in the semester. Then make adjustments.

❏ Handle any troublemakers professionally.

❏ Teach your students how to keep discussions going deeper through critical thinking questions. Model critical thinking questions regularly.

❏ Incorporate various techniques for discussion.

❏ Incorporate various techniques to solicit questions from your students.

❏ Get your students to participate actively in each class.

❏ Use multiple means of presenting information (visual, auditory, kinesthetic).

❏ Communicate your enthusiasm for your subject area daily.

# *Active Teaching and Learning*

## Helping Students Learn to Learn

One of the greatest gifts you can give students is to help them learn how to learn. Many students come to college with no real idea of some of the basic techniques that will help them succeed. Even some really top students can flounder in college because high school was so easy for them they didn't learn study skills.

It's a good idea to review study techniques in your class during the first week. The ideas below are from educational psychology research and are sound approaches to helping students learn how to learn. Go over each of these topics.

## Daily Study

It seems obvious to us, but inexperienced students frequently procrastinate. They don't realize that 30 minutes a day adds up. I joke with students and tell them to haul their psychology book everywhere so they can read at red lights and in the bathroom. They groan, but I make my point: a little bit at a time and it's done.

Emphasize how important it is to study when alert, not exhausted. Studying when exhausted is usually ineffective. Students wonder why they read the whole chapter and don't remember anything! When doing "zombie reading," they can't process the material.

Share the Premack Principle: "Eat your peas before you can have dessert." This principle of operant conditioning links a less desirable behavior to a more rewarding behavior. (This principle was identified by David Premack in 1965, so it bears his name, but parents have been using it forever.) Talk with your students about self-discipline, attaining goals, and using the Premack principle to build self-discipline. If they learn to study before they play, then they can play without nagging guilt and really enjoy it—and do better in their courses.

## Reading the Material

Advise students to *preview*, to flip through the chapter or article first, reading the headings and the captions of photos, examining the charts, and reading any summary information. This preview orients the student to the material and helps them make connections when they do a more thorough reading.

Suggest that students ask and answer questions as they read. A good textbook might ask questions along each page edge, you could provide some questions, or there may be a study guide available for your textbook.

Encourage students to reflect as they read, to try to apply what they are reading to something they already know. This is a vital skill for remembering information. The more connections, the more easily memory storage and retrieval happen.

Explain the *serial position effect*: we remember the beginning and the end of information more readily than the middle. Thus, breaking chapters up into small segments, rather than reading all at once, creates more beginnings and ends, so we will remember more.

Encourage distributed practice (little bits over time) because it works better than cramming (lots at once). If you think about long-term memory as a swimming pool, cramming puts information into the shallow end where it can leap out quickly, while distributed practice puts information closer to the deep end where it has a chance to remain. Distributed practice allows time for the mind to process information.

Students should highlight and underline—but not too much. Highlighting means marking the most important things, not almost everything. Less highlighting actually correlates to higher learning. Students are forced to identify the main issues as they read. Then, when they review, the points stand out.

## *Memorizing*

Remember: your job isn't to give out information; it's to facilitate learning. So whatever you can do to help your students learn will eventually make both them and you more successful.

Learning often involves memorizing. Reading is not memorizing. This is a key point to share with your students. They should not expect to know information just because they read it. They have to actively put it into their memories.

Help your students learn the principle of overlearning, which is simply to go over and over and over the material way past the point at which you know it in order to make it yours.

Wonderful tools for overlearning are flash cards. People have made fun of flash cards but that's because too much schooling has focused exclusively on facts. We need some facts in order to build the higher levels of cognition and flash cards are good tools for learning them. However, flash cards are good for more than facts. They can hold explanations, critical questions, and so on.

The Web has fabulous resources on memory techniques, for free. Numerous sites explain the peg method, loci method, and other techniques. Find several techniques and then, as an in-class activity, have students actively try them. You will be teaching them to memorize while they memorize your material.

## Mind Mapping

Yes, students should be taking notes in class. Yes, some students will persist in sitting there staring at you even when you say, "You might want to take notes on this part." I think this is sometimes because they haven't a clue how to take notes. (You can encourage them to take notes by awarding points.) Teach your students how to take notes; it will be worth your time and effort.

The classic I, II, III, IV method of taking notes is not always the best. We were all taught to outline by the standard old method: I, II, III, IV, a., b., c. Our teachers told us that if there wasn't enough information for a "b" we couldn't have just an "a." Many students try to take notes with this old method.

But there's a problem with outlining with the old method: it doesn't fit the way our minds actually work. We aren't totally linear thinkers. We think in patterns. We think in images. Our brains love images, pictures, visuals. We can remember a good picture far easier than an outline. And many times—gasp!—we have "a" in our thoughts without "b."

Teach your students mind-mapping. It works better for many students.

Mind mapping takes what we know about memory and the brain and turns it into a satisfying note-taking system that truly makes sense. When students use color and draw little doodles of their thoughts within the mind map, it works even better.

Here's the only problem with mind mapping. People are reluctant to learn something new, even when it will help them learn faster and remember more. Yes, research in mind mapping does find those results. Now if we can just get people to do it!

### Introducing Mind Maps to Students

A mind map is a diagram used to link words and concepts and facts to a central concept or word or idea. You can use it to visualize concepts and ideas and show how they interrelate. You can also use it to generate ideas. You organize concepts and facts and words spatially and draw lines to indicate connections among them, forming branches and groups.

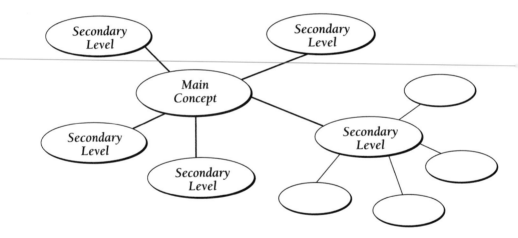

## Teaching Critical Thinking Skills

It's a classic lament around the faculty copy machine: "These students can't think!" Well, maybe not yet—but they can learn to think. And it's part of your job to teach students to think critically within your field.

There's a little book that can help you do so: *The Miniature Guide to Critical Thinking Concepts and Tools* by Dr. Richard Paul and Dr. Linda Elder

(Foundation for Critical Thinking, 2001). It's so good, in fact, that I strongly recommend you consider it as a required text in some of your courses.

*The Miniature Guide* is pocketsize, only 19 pages, and inexpensive too! But it really covers such a broad sweep of information that it will help you improve your assessment, your discussion techniques, and your questioning skills and it will enable your students to approach their lives more thoughtfully. I love the entire *Miniature Guide*, but there is one page I use religiously and require my students to have out in front of them during group discussions. I have reproduced this page (with permission of the authors) on the following page.

### Keys to Developing Critical Thinking Skills

Model critical thinking for your students obviously. Don't expect them all to pick out your thought processes, especially if your conclusions are in any way opposed to their preconceptions. (They will have roadblocks up.)

Develop sets of questions based on the Clarity–Fairness considerations that apply to the concepts you are teaching. At the beginning, point the questions out as students follow along with your thoughts.

Have students develop their own sets of questions in groups, based on the Clarity–Fairness considerations, for a specific issue or case study. Then have groups exchange questions and answer them. This helps students internalize the benefits of thinking critically and makes discussions deeper and livelier. Students will have to think before speaking because other students will challenge their assertions. This is real progress!

Don't give up! Some students actually resist thinking critically or challenging others with anything but opinions unsupported by facts. Keep at it!

## *Dynamic Direct Instruction (Horror! A Lecture!)*

This point is vital: Many college instructors think a lot about their content, but put little energy into thinking about how they will help students remember and learn that content. But planning for student learning makes the difference between *teaching* and simply *presenting* information. You have to spend significant energy planning instruction if you want to be superior at teaching.

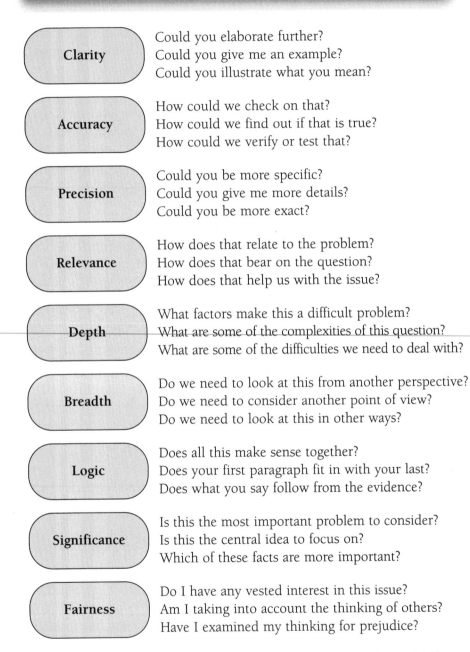

| | |
|---|---|
| **Clarity** | Could you elaborate further?<br>Could you give me an example?<br>Could you illustrate what you mean? |
| **Accuracy** | How could we check on that?<br>How could we find out if that is true?<br>How could we verify or test that? |
| **Precision** | Could you be more specific?<br>Could you give me more details?<br>Could you be more exact? |
| **Relevance** | How does that relate to the problem?<br>How does that bear on the question?<br>How does that help us with the issue? |
| **Depth** | What factors make this a difficult problem?<br>What are some of the complexities of this question?<br>What are some of the difficulties we need to deal with? |
| **Breadth** | Do we need to look at this from another perspective?<br>Do we need to consider another point of view?<br>Do we need to look at this in other ways? |
| **Logic** | Does all this make sense together?<br>Does your first paragraph fit in with your last?<br>Does what you say follow from the evidence? |
| **Significance** | Is this the most important problem to consider?<br>Is this the central idea to focus on?<br>Which of these facts are more important? |
| **Fairness** | Do I have any vested interest in this issue?<br>Am I taking into account the thinking of others?<br>Have I examined my thinking for prejudice? |

*The Miniature Guide to Critical Thinking Concepts and Tools* by Dr. Richard Paul and Dr. Linda Elder, p. 9, Foundation for Critical Thinking, *www.criticalthinking.org.* Used with permission.

Lecture has gotten a bad rap. I sometimes think that if I read one more article about moving away from the "sage on the stage" to the "guide on the side" I'll regurgitate—and it won't be knowledge!

Students expect their instructors to be knowledge experts. Students want a certain amount of lecture—just not *all* lecture. Classes that involve *all* peer or small group interaction are generally unpopular among the better students, who want to learn from *you*, the expert, not from other students who know no more than they do. Yes, some students want lectures so they can sleep in the back of the class and not expend themselves. But far more students want them because they want to learn something from an expert. They are weary of their peers' opinions.

A good lecture from a knowledgeable, motivating, fabulous speaker is a work of art. (It's just that so many of us don't realize we aren't Picasso.)

## The Design of Good, Direct Instruction (Sample Lecture Punctuated with Activity)

1. Start with a little review to place students in the context of what has come before. "Yesterday we left off with classical conditioning ... drooling dogs. You will remember that classical conditioning is a basic type of learning involving ...blah, blah, blah." Just hit the highlights for three to five minutes. Don't review the whole lesson.

2. Next, preview what you will be covering in this period. "Today we are going to ...." One great way to do this is to write your agenda on the board before class starts and mark off each item as you finish it.

   ❑ Review of classical conditioning components (5 minutes)
   ❑ Overview of operant conditioning (15–20 minutes)
   ❑ Activity on operant conditioning (15 minutes)
   ❑ Review activity (10 minutes)
   ❑ Break
   ❑ Quiz (10 minutes)

3. Show the objectives for the day. "After today you should be able to ...." 1, 2, 3, 4."

4. Then, lecture. *But* your material must be highly organized *and* you should lecture no more than 20 minutes at a time. Adults can focus for only about 20 minutes, tops. Then their minds start to wander.

   - Tie the information to previously learned concepts. Point out the connections.
   - Use visuals like charts and graphs.
   - Give multiple examples. Use student majors and areas of interest in your examples, if at all possible.
   - Foreshadow connections to what will be coming, if appropriate.

5. After you lecture, engage your students in a review of the information just presented. Use one of the active techniques listed later in this book that don't require too much movement, like Pair Share.

6. Ask for questions. Ascertain if students understand. You might need to ask questions.

7. Give the students an opportunity to actively practice what you just taught, with a meaningful, challenging activity. "Using operant conditioning, plan a program to train a dolphin to jump through a hoop. Use the correct terms."

8. Then, process the activity. Ask probing questions about their results and how they worked to produce those results. Give feedback.

After processing the activity, move into your next lecture (next objective) or review the material, whichever is still needed.

The key to this technique of direct instruction is that the combination of lecture and activity maintains motivation for most students and helps them learn and remember.

# Active Learning:
# The Philosophy and the Drawbacks

## The Philosophy

For way too many years, college education has involved students primarily as passive learners. Straight lectures have been the favored mode of instruction and there was little if any active in-class student participation unless it involved a laboratory experience. Lecture worked well for a minority of students, but it left many others struggling and bored.

Now that we know so much more about the brain, information processing, memory, and learning, we have other, better ways than straight lecture to reach more students. We now know that the more actively students are engaged while they are processing information, the more likely they are to understand and retain it. This doesn't mean they have to be active physically, up running around, but they do have to be active mentally.

Active teaching and learning are part of a revolution in teaching. It began in the lower grades and in the corporate training classrooms and has finally worked its way into colleges and universities. Good instructors need to master some basic active teaching techniques so their students will be learning actively in the classroom.

## The Drawbacks

Unfortunately, college students still expect straight lectures as the primary mode of "information transmittal." Some are actually reluctant to engage in active learning techniques and need to be informed about why these techniques are worth their effort. Bright students, in particular, may be opposed to learning with/from peers. Don't drop all lecture from courses with a lot of content; punctuate lectures with activities.

Your colleagues may or may not be familiar with active learning techniques, so they will react to your use of active teaching in various ways, supportive or not. Some colleagues may have adopted active learning as a positive venture but are personally using stupid activities and busywork under the guise of active learning. If you have colleagues who use activities that are "cute" rather than challenging, this will have turned students off to the concept and you will have to work twice as hard to win them over.

Also, active learning techniques used in corporate environments may not work well in your classroom. Corporate training happens in brief spurts, not over an entire semester. Corporate trainers usually have control over their space for the duration of the training, while college instructors share space and cannot move everything around without impacting others. Use resources intended for corporate training to get ideas for activities, but be aware you'll have to modify training activities for your students.

## Grounding Principles

### What We Know About Learning

We know that extremely stressful situations increase anxiety and inhibit learning. You need to find the right balance between stress and challenge, putting your students into a situation that stretches them but doesn't threaten them. This might be the difference between giving a difficult problem to a group and giving the problem to an individual, whose self-esteem is then on the line in front of others.

We know that being emotionally involved heightens our chances of learning more. Why? We're probably more alert and attention is the critical first step to learning. Without attention, there's little or no potential for learning. Emotions also trigger a whole sequence of chemicals in the body and brain that have powerful effects. But avoid fear, which triggers fight-or-flight responses—not exactly conducive to higher-order thinking. Emotions are part of us; you can't separate them from learning.

We know that unpleasant emotional experiences with a subject can impede our ability to approach it. The math-class-from-hell in high school conditions feelings about math in college, "anchoring" a new math course to the bad feelings from math in the past. How can you help students overcome their negative emotional experiences?

We know that our bodies are part of the learning process. When students are dehydrated, poorly fed, exhausted, or otherwise challenged physiologically, learning is harder. Talk to them about this. In addition, involve the body in learning activities—movement and physical engagement are ways to facilitate learning.

We know that we like meaning. Our brain craves it. Our brain seeks patterns and connections. Unrelated bits of information are hard to memorize and harder to recall. So, the more connections we make between old and new information, the better our chances of helping our students deeply understand, process, and recall the new information. Involving the body in creating meaning also helps learning.

We know that we learn with our whole brain, not just the "left side" or the "right side," although certain processes are more "focused" in one hemisphere or the other. We need to engage both sides, the whole brain, in as many ways as possible. Using a wide variety of active teaching and active learning techniques can do this.

We know that whatever is personally meaningful is processed differently and will be retained. We have different types of memory and can memorize an amazing array of information, retaining it for brief or long periods of time, depending upon how we process it. We can memorize a lot with our rote memory areas, but information learned this way generally is not retained for long. If we want learning, not just memorization, then we need to make information meaningful and put it into context for our students.

## The Value of Images, Stories, and Fun

Our brains love to process images. Think about how much available information is contained in a single "snapshot" image and how many words you would have to use to fully describe the same scene. ("A picture is worth a thousand words.") Images help us process and help us remember. We've been using our brains to process images a lot longer than we've been using them to process the written word. Instructors can use this natural talent for remembering images to help students learn and remember.

### Using Images

As you walk through a theory or concept, illustrate it with visual images on an overhead. Model this technique for your students.

PowerPoint might be clean, techie, and all the rage—but instructors who can draw cartoon figures and images to illustrate a lecture as it unfolds will capture the attention of students far better.

Eventually, have individuals or groups develop images that explain a concept or theory and present it to the class.

Emphasize the importance of including images in mind maps.

Imagery research supports this technique: use of images may improve not only immediate recall, but long-term retention as well.

## Using Stories

Stories are "auditory images": The storyteller paints the images with words and we complete them in our brains. A really well told story can be an effective way to help students remember.

Not everyone is a story-teller. If you have no natural tendencies in this direction, don't use stories without a lot of practice. You don't want to lull your students to sleep.

## Using Games

Games are especially good when reviewing for a test. You can cover the material and, at the same time, reduce anxiety.

Games with a point are fun: they make class feel less serious—and this can be a really good thing. If they aren't going to improve learning, however, don't use them!

Jeopardy is a popular review game. The free template with clapping and music you can download from the Web works very well and is easy to modify for any subject area.

You can convert almost any old card or board game or any TV game show. I developed a game I called "Old Psychologist," patterned after Old Maid. It works fairly well, but I need to refine it. You'll want to pilot your new games before using them.

Try point basketball. All you need is a ball, a hoop, and some questions. Divide the students into groups. Each group draws a question; if the members can answer it correctly in 20 seconds, they get to throw the ball for two points. The highest-scoring team at the end wins something— food, drinks, extra credit points, or whatever.

Games create competition, but this is very different from the atmosphere of a competitive classroom. No review game competition has ever backfired on me. Instead, they've generated lots of laughter, good-natured ribbing, and higher test scores for some students.

# Critical Aspects of Good Active Learning Activities

Here are eight essentials of effective active learning activities:

- They relate directly to the lesson at hand.
- They require critical thinking.
- They are enjoyable and interesting, but not silly or childish.
- They challenge the students.
- They add real value for the students.
- The students can finish them and get feedback within the same class period.
- The instructor uses them judiciously—not the same activity for every situation.

# Active Learning Technique One— Lecture Interrupting

While giving information out in a mini-lecture (remember: no more than 20 minutes), you want the students actively engaged and processing the information. There are several "little" techniques for ensuring they will stay attentive and learn. Set very brief time limits with these so you can move on and not get bogged down.

## Pair Share and Application

Stop your lecture. Ask the students to pair up and then have one partner explain to the other what you just said (understanding level of Bloom) and give an example from his or her own life (application level of Bloom). The first few times you do this, you'll startle a lot of students whose minds may have been wandering. But if you use this activity enough and follow it up occasionally with a written product, eventually students will pay more attention to your lectures.

Here's an example in psychology. After explaining the difference between a schema and a script, you have the students pair up and then you ask one partner to explain to the other the difference between a schema and a script and then give an example of each from his or her life. An extension of this would be to have each student write down the example given by his or her partner and then explain (in writing) why it is a schema or a script. Give points for a good job.

Switch pairings occasionally. This develops some low-level peer pressure to process information attentively and gets each student to meet more of his or her classmates and hear new views.

### Instant Memory Technique
Stop your lecture. Have the students form pairs or mini-groups and develop a technique for remembering the concept(s) you've just covered. Students will usually work out a memory technique that helps them to understand the material. Have students share their techniques and they will be helping the other students learn the concept.

### Similes
Stop your lecture. Ask the students to form mini-groups to build similes (or metaphors) for a concept. Similes: X is like Y. Metaphors compare things but without "like": "crystallized intelligence is a rock and fluid intelligence is water.") Then have the groups explain their answers. This works equally well as a group or individual effort. It can also serve as a formative assessment if the students write out their similes and pass them in.

## Active Learning Technique Two—Build It

Back in elementary school, when you had to build a model of soil erosion with real water and real dirt, your teacher was on to something—and you probably remember the principles of soil erosion to this day. We can use the building technique extremely effectively in the college environment as well. The appeal of the building technique is that it's kinesthetic, it's a whole-body approach, it's group work, it's fun, it's challenging, and there are positive interactions with peers. Here are some suggestions.

### Building Processes
Whole classes can act out a complex process. One of the best examples of this I have seen is a demonstration of how information gets from one com-

puter to another over the Internet. The technical college faculty member I have seen use this technique comes prepared with big bold signs (such as "IP") for each stage of the process, which students can hang around their necks. While explaining the process, as he adds the next component he adds a student to the living process model. Eventually, the room is connected with students holding a rope connecting all the components in a series. Then students volunteer to verbally "walk" through the process. Or, in a round-robin, the first student in line says what he or she does, the second student takes the "message" from there. This activity has been very effective and is a good example of a "build it" active learning technique. These types of processes can also be modeled with simple slips of paper taped on desks.

## Building Models

You can engage students in building models in groups. Anatomy is a subject area that seems to be straight boring memorization in so many classes, but it doesn't have to be. Clay to the rescue! After the anatomy instructor goes over the components of the knee, student groups can build a knee out of clay and put toothpicks in the component parts. Then, groups can rotate and identify each part marked by the toothpicks. The act of shaping the parts with your own hands is quite different from just looking at a picture or even handling an expensive plastic model. Physical modeling, of course, will work well for a variety of classes. Put a time limit on construction to keep the class moving.

## Reconstructing

Some subject areas, like English composition, lend themselves to the activity of reconstruction. To demonstrate how coherence works to develop "flow" in a paragraph, I pair up my students and give each pair a paragraph cut up into sentences. In a tightly coherent paragraph, the sentences should fit together so well that the students can put them into my original order. The students attempt to reconstruct my paragraph, discussing why they put the sentences in the order they did.

I have a few such samples, illustrating different methods of developing coherence. Next, I have students write paragraphs and then cut them up into sentences for the other pairs to reconstruct. Invariably students have trouble putting one another's initial paragraphs back together in the correct order. This difficulty generates a lot of discussion. Students then get the chance to revise their paragraphs and cut them up again.

I use this technique several times during the course. My students learn about coherence because they need to revise their paragraphs until other students can reconstruct them consistently. Students generally find this a lot of fun. They take it as a challenge to write so clearly that anyone can reconstruct their paragraphs. You can reconstruct in many content areas.

## Active Learning Technique Three— What Do You Think, Dr. Dewey?

This fun, fabulous activity can be used to generate deeper understanding of a particular topic or to review facts and figures before a test. Either way, it is fairly non-threatening and I've never had a class where the students didn't enjoy it. Some profit more than others, but that usually has to do with how serious the students are. If you can't handle a certain amount of good-natured "off-target" comments, you probably won't want to use this technique. The instructor can keep it more serious via the questions tolerated and the intended outcome communicated. This is a perfect technique for using props—old-fashioned hats from the local thrift store add a special measure of fun and encourage participation. This technique never fails to bring out the "ham" in a few students.

But don't underestimate its power to also promote learning. It can test understanding and it's a good formative assessment technique.

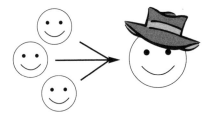

*Step one.* Have the students generate questions. "What if the great educator John Dewey were here today? What you like to ask Dr. Dewey?" Have students (either individually or in small groups) generate questions to ask a specific person whose theories are covered in their readings (e.g., Sigmund Freud, Noam Chomsky). The person can be alive or dead. I usually gather the questions in a box to retain some control and add some of my own. You can collect questions one day, preview them, and hand only the worthy ones back to small groups on the next class period when you'll complete this activity. That works well too.

*Step two.* Get a volunteer to be the honored guest. (A good hat will help get volunteers!) Explain that this is the "mouth" of "Dr. Dewey" and the volunteer can only repeat what her or his "brains" say. "Dr. Dewey" sits in front of the class.

*Step three.* Get volunteers or appoint three "brain cells." Depending upon your outcomes, these three students can have their notes with them or not. These individuals huddle behind Dr. Dewey, ready to provide him answers.

*Step four.* Ask the best questions. Don't allow "Dr. Dewey" to generate input. The answers must come from the brains, whispering behind her or him. This should remain fun and productive. This also works best if the instructor is good at thinking on the spot and can generate deeper questions out of "Dr. Dewey's" responses. You can turn to the class for help if the brain cells get stumped. Have students keep their critical thinking pages out so they can generate better questions.

*Step five.* Brain transplant. Part way through the activity, ask for a brain transplant. Replace the three brain cells with three fresh brain cells. If you select at random, it works well to keep all the students on their toes.

## *Active Learning Technique Four— What Do You Think, Noted Panelists?*

This active learning technique is a take-off on Dr. Dewey. It involves more students at once and can get into the dynamics of a debate quickly. Be sure to set the ground rules in both these techniques: opinions must be based on facts.

*Step one.* Have the students, individually or in small groups, generate questions on a specific issue. Example: "If we had several noted psychologists here, three Freudians and three Humanists, what would you like to ask them?" If you want to explore a specific issue, like the roots of mental illness and how it can be "cured," then be sure to specify. Collect the questions. Again, you can go through them ahead of time and add some of your own to be sure to cover certain points.

*Step two.* Get volunteers to serve on the panels. Set up chairs or tables and chairs so there are two panels, facing each other.

*Step three.* Appoint a moderator or take the role yourself. If you appoint one, choose wisely. The moderator fields the questions.

*Step four.* Have fun! Make sure the members of a panel agree on the answer before they give it. Don't let one or two people take over. Have students keep their critical thinking pages out and use them to generate deeper and deeper questions.

## *Active Learning Technique Five— Nominal Group*

This is a technique used in many meetings run by corporate trainers, but we have found it to be quite effective in the college classroom—with the right question. Having just the right question is the key.

Nominal group techniques work best for evaluative or informed-opinion types of items, rather than facts. Two examples would be "What are the most important things for a teacher to do on the first day?" and "What are the chief things to keep in mind as you are preparing to lead a group in strategic planning?" These are the types of questions that work. Nominal group also works for developing class goals, helping to select topics to cover, or deciding on types of assignments. Students love it and it gets everyone involved. This is a very powerful tool *if* you choose the right question to answer. Keep control of the time!

Benefits: This is a very inclusive procedure. It involves lots of discussion within groups. The students practice interpersonal skills. It is aimed at Bloom's highest levels of the cognitive domain, evaluation, and synthesis (depending upon your question).

*Step one: brainstorm phase.* Present your question and break students into small groups to answer it using brainstorming fashion. Have each group generate 10 ideas (more or less) in a specific amount of time.

*Step two: prioritization phase.* Now, tell the groups to prioritize their brainstormed answers, putting them in order of most important to least important.

*Step three: sharing-top-three phase.* Give a bold marker and large sticky notes or sheets of paper to each group. Have them write down, in only two to five words, their top three ideas, one to a note or sheet, so everyone can read them. Have all the groups tape their lists of top three ideas to the board.

*Step four: categorizing phase.* As a large group, put the top threes into categories.

*Step five: sharing ideas four through six.* Back in their small groups, have students write down the next three items from their prioritization lists, again only one idea to a sheet of paper, and put them up on the board. Again, as a large group, categorize them.

*Step six: anything-else phase.* Back in the small groups, allow students to add any idea they feel wasn't covered that is truly extremely important to include, one idea to a note or sheet. Categorize these remaining ideas with the others already on the board.

*Step seven.* Process your results as a large group.

## Active Learning Technique Six— "Apply-Sheets" and Scenarios

"Worksheets" have an awful stigma, so call them something else—"apply-sheets." When you generate your own "apply-sheets" for a specific topic covered in your 20-minute interactive lecture, they are excellent active learning tools. Scenarios or case studies are equally effective as apply-sheets.

You need to plan ahead and copy ahead. Make sure you design these sheets or scenarios to focus directly on the objective at hand, giving students a chance to immediately apply what they just learned.

The primary cognitive levels here are usually analysis and application, so of course students have to know and understand the information first. Don't just focus your apply-sheets and scenarios on rote memorization. Go higher. Students like working through challenging, interesting problems in groups. Note that the emphasis is on challenge. They hate apply-sheets that only ask for simple, easy answers. You want students discussing and wrestling with the information.

*Lecture* ⟶ *Apply-Sheet/ Scenario in Groups* ⟶ *Follow-up* ⟶ *Discussion* ⟶ *Maybe Back to Lecture*

## Examples from a psychology class:

**Situation:** You have just covered Kohlberg's Stages of Moral Reasoning.

**Apply-Sheet:** You pass out a real Kohlbergian dilemma. Students must solve the dilemma in a small group for each level of moral reasoning.

**Situation:** You have just covered classical conditioning.

**Apply-Sheet:** You pass out a scenario about a student who has high test anxiety. Students must work through the elements to identify the classical conditioning components and give suggestions for extinguishing the behavior.

**Situation:** You have just covered the information-processing model of memory.

**Apply-Sheet:** You give students a list of sensations, memories, and thoughts to place into the right section of the information-processing model.

**Situation:** You have covered the major perspectives in modern psychology.

· **Apply-Sheet:** You give students a scenario involving domestic violence. They must put themselves into the position of a group of psychologists giving expert testimony in a court case involving a man who is beating his wife and the wife who is continually returning. From the various perspectives of modern psychology, they need to posit explanations for both behaviors and recommend the kind of treatment that will likely help stop the cycle of violence.

**Benefits:** You can make your own "small bite" apply-sheets and scenarios to relate to your current lesson/objective. What you can do is limited only by your imagination. Students love applying information immediately, which solidifies their understanding and illuminates their misconceptions. Great group interaction, too!

## Active Learning Technique Seven— Multipurpose Activities

### Pros/Cons, Similarities/Differences, Many/Few

I develop these general activities and keep a supply in the class boxes. Their usefulness is pretty obvious. You verbalize the concepts, time periods, theories, etc. to compare and students write them in. These are good active learning activities for groups or pairs, but done individually they are also powerful formative assessments of the current level of student understanding. Samples are shown on page 114.

Topic:_____ *[Nuclear Energy]* _____

| Pros | Cons |
|------|------|
|      |      |

Compare:_____ *[Civil War]* __and___ *[Revolution]* ___

| Similarities | Differences |
|--------------|-------------|
|              |             |

Question:_____ *[Ways to stop slope soil erosion in desert terrains]* _____

| Brainstorm Several Ideas Here | Select Two— What Makes Them Most Viable? |
|-------------------------------|------------------------------------------|
|                               |                                          |
|                               |                                          |

# *Active Learning Technique Eight— Jigsaw Method*

This method of engaging students in designing their own learning can be highly effective in the college environment. Just do not overuse it or students will feel you aren't doing your own job.

I have seen student test scores jump quite phenomenally after a whole class period was devoted to using the jigsaw method. Again, your brightest students can get frustrated with this method if you use it too much, but the students who struggle to find time to study or who have a harder time processing what they read will benefit—sometimes dramatically. This is a tried-and-true method used extensively in the lower grades. It keeps students actively engaged, gets them to work together with purpose, and helps them learn various study methods and take responsibility for learning. I spice it up on occasion by offering to give five extra points if the whole class gets 100% on the test that comes after the jigsaw, four extra points if the most missed is one, etc. I usually test right after using the jigsaw, particularly if the class period is a four-hour block.

*Step one.* Prepare study sheets ahead of time with the terms and concepts the students need to understand. Don't include answers, just the terms and concepts. Divide the terms and concepts equally among four to six sheets of different colored paper. How many sets you make depends on the size of your class and the time you want to allow for the jigsaw. Make several copies of each set.

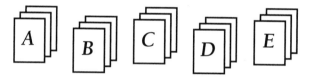

*Step two.* Form initial groups. Pass out your sheets in class, distributing the same number of each color or as close as possible. Explain the jigsaw method. Then have all students with the same color form a group. The job of each group is to look up the information on its study sheet and to make sure that every member of the group thoroughly understands each term or concept. Each will be teaching that group's terms and concepts to members of other groups later. Give them time to learn their material.

*Step three.* Form mixed groups. Hopefully you will have only one student with each color group, but this varies with class size. You *must* have at least one member from each initial group, of course, because each initial group has unique information. Now, students teach their info to each other.

## Checklist: Active Teaching and Learning Techniques

❏ Review with your students during the first week tips on how to read a college text.

❏ Emphasize good study techniques the first day.

❏ Model critical thinking very obviously.

❏ Adopt *The Miniature Guide to Critical Thinking* (if appropriate to subject—as it usually is).

❏ Develop sets of questions for lessons ahead of time, based on critical thinking criteria. Do *not* wing it!

❏ Plan activities in which students form groups to develop sets of critical thinking questions for students in other groups to answer.

❏ Design good, direct instruction for some lessons.

❏ Introduce students to the concept of active learning. Explain their role, your role, and why active learning can help them learn faster and remember more.

❏ Develop several mind maps of complex concepts—some to pass out, some to use as blank models while teaching mind mapping.

❏ Introduce the students to several memory techniques.

❏ Plan times to have students develop and share their own memory techniques.

❏ Lead students to the Web sites that teach good memorization skills.

❏ Plan lessons to incorporate images, stories, and humor.

❏ Design a couple of games for review sessions or download the template for Jeopardy.

❏ Plan lessons to incorporate active learning and map out when to use the different techniques.

❑ Design apply-sheets for difficult concepts, make copies, and have them ready.

❑ Design multipurpose apply-sheets, make copies, and store them in the box.

❑ Examine each of your activities for the following qualities:

- The challenge level is substantial.
- It covers a major point or objective you want to emphasize.
- It requires critical thinking.
- It can be finished and discussed during the same class period.
- There's nothing frivolous, time-wasting, or cute.

# Communication

## Miscellaneous Communication Tips

**With students:**

- Return phone calls and e-mails promptly.

- Be available before and after class.

- Keep your stated office hours. It is very frustrating for students to try to catch an instructor during their posted office hours only to find the office locked (you didn't come in) or empty (you're at the copy machine or talking with friends).

- Keep your office door open when talking with students.

- Keep records of any student correspondence so you have a paper trail.

- Keep file folders and papers after the semester ends, in case a student disputes a grade. Tell students how long you will keep them. Check whether your department has a policy on keeping student work. If a student challenges a grade and you no longer have the assignments and tests to support the grade, it would be a serious problem, especially for an adjunct or new instructor. Check!

- Give weekly feedback in each student's file, if at all possible.

**With administrators:**

- Keep in e-mail contact with your faculty mentor and with your supervisor. Tell them the positives that are happening. Get help with problems.

- When you are an adjunct, remind the "powers" early, more than once and in writing, that you want more classes next semester or next year. Keep visible if you want to keep viable.

- Keep a paper trail of administrative correspondence so "he-said, she-said" is minimized on important issues.

- Warn administrators if there is a serious issue. They hate surprises.

- After meeting with administrators, write to the parties involved to thank them for the meeting and reiterate point by point your understanding of what was discussed. Invite them to clarify if they had a different recollection. Memories can be fuzzy for anyone.

- Ask administrators for help when you need the Big Guns, like support with a cheating issue you are uncomfortable handling alone.

**With colleagues:**

- Don't be in a big rush to get in and out each day. Make friends with other faculty: chat with them, ask them questions, get to know them personally. They are your best allies and best problem-solvers.

- Be sure to communicate all the good times you experience. Build collegial friendships.

- Faculty friendships are also a good avenue to additional appointments for adjuncts or recommendations for full-timers looking for work elsewhere. For adjuncts, the faculty around you will likely be on any selection committee for full-time jobs at your institution and they know administrators and faculty at other institutions. Let them know you are looking for work!

- Help your colleagues with projects: assessment plans, surveys, research, etc.

- Attend all meetings in your department that you can. Participate. Ask first, however. Sometimes adjuncts are not welcome during discussions of sensitive issues like hiring. In general, though, participation in meetings and school events is a wise idea.

# Final Words

Get to know your students. It will not be very long before they are running the world. Teach them well. Help them learn respect by respecting them. Help them develop critical thinking skills so they can make better decisions for themselves and our planet throughout their lives.

More communication is better than less communication.

When you make mistakes, admit them. When you don't know, say so. We all respect people who can say, "Good question! I don't know the answer to that, but I'll try to find out by our next class."

Whether you are an adjunct or a full-timer, teaching is an important profession. Helping others learn is a privilege and an honor. Chant that to yourself on the lean days; celebrate it on the good days.

There will be ample good days. Enjoy.

# Good Resources for Instructors

### Bloom's Taxonomy

There are many great resources on Bloom's taxonomy, but here is one Web site that links to numerous other Bloom sites and also includes links on critical and creative thinking:

*eduscapes.com/tap/topic69.htm*

### Critical Thinking

Fabulous site on critical thinking, with many books and articles of immense value:

*criticalthinking.org*

### Further Reading

Anderson, Lorin, and David R. Krathwohl (eds.). 2001. *A taxonomy for learning, teaching, and assessing: A revision of Bloom's Taxonomy of educational objectives.* Boston: Allyn & Bacon.

Angelo, Thomas A., and K. Patricia Cross. 2005. *Classroom assessment techniques: A handbook for college teachers,* rev. ed. Hoboken, NJ: John Wiley & Sons.

Bloom, Benjamin S. (ed.) 1956. *Taxonomy of educational objectives: The classification of educational goals.* New York: David McKay.

Brinkley, Alan, Betty Dessants, Michael Flamm, Cynthia Fleming, Charles Forcey, and Eric Rothschild. 1999. *The Chicago handbook for teachers: A practical guide to the college classroom.* Chicago: University of Chicago Press.

Burton, Steven J., Richard R. Sudweeks, Paul F. Merrill, and Bud Wood. 2001. *How to prepare better multiple-choice test items: Guidelines for university faculty.* Available online at: testingbyu.edu/info/handbooks/betteritems.pdf.

Davis, Barbara Gross. 1993. *Tools for teaching.* San Francisco: Jossey-Bass.

Jensen, Eric P. 2000. *Brain-based learning: the new science of teaching and training,* rev. ed. San Diego, CA: The Brain Store®.

Magnan, Robert. 1989. *147 Practical Tips for teaching professors,* rev. ed. Madison, WI: Atwood Publishing.

McKeachie, Wilbert J., and Marilla Svinicki (eds.). 2005. *McKeachie's teaching tips: Strategies, research, and theory for college and university teachers,* 12th ed. Boston: Houghton Mifflin.

Meier, David. 2000. *The accelerated learning handbook: A creative guide to designing and delivering faster, more effective training programs.* New York: McGraw-Hill.

Paul, Richard, and Linda Elder. 2001. *The miniature guide to critical thinking: Concepts and tools.* Dillon Beach, CA: Foundation for Critical Thinking.

Pintrich, Paul R., and Dale H. Schunk. 1996. *Motivation in education: Theory, research, and applications.* Englewood Cliffs, NJ: Merrill.

Wigfield, Allan, and Jacqueline S. Eccles (eds.). 2001. *Development of achievement motivation.* Orlando, FL: Academic Press.

Wood, Robert, and Albert Bandura. 1989. Social cognitive theory of organizational management. *Academy of Management Review,* 14:361-384.

Woolfolk, Anita E. 2006. *Educational psychology,* 10th ed. Boston: Allyn & Bacon.

*[Note: Woolfolk (2006) is a good textbook citing way too many educational psychology research studies for anyone's sane use but a terrific resource.]*

## Patricia Linehan

Patricia Linehan has been teaching at the college level either full or part-time since 1984. She received her Masters in English from Colorado State University in 1983 and Ph.D. in Educational Psychology from Purdue University in 1994. She taught adjunct for several colleges and universities including Indiana University, St. Mary's (MN), Minnesota State University-Mankato, and William Penn. Dr. Linehan served as the Director of Assessment for William Penn University in Iowa and the Dean of Research, Planning and Development for South Central College in Minnesota. She has given dozens of workshops on assessment techniques and active teaching to faculty and staff, and currently enjoys teaching Psychology and English at South Central College. The wife of a retired military officer and mother to three teenage sons, when not teaching or writing you will find her tending enormous gardens or learning to spin and weave, surrounded by a large assortment of cats and dogs.

# Notes